8/95

WITHDRAWN

Vegetarianism
A History

by
Jon Gregerson

JAIN PUBLISHING COMPANY
Fremont, California

Library of Congress Cataloging-in-Publication Data

Gregerson, Jon.
    Vegetarianism, a history / by Jon Gregerson.
      p.   cm.
    Includes bibliographical references and index.
    ISBN 0-87573-030-2
    1. Vegetarianism—History.   I. Title.
TX392.G73   1994
613.2'62—dc20   94-10691
                                                  CIP

Contents

Introduction

Our purpose in this study is to provide a much needed history of vegetarianism from a strictly vegetarian perspective, relating its development in both East and West to the particular historical periods and cultures in which it evolved as well as to the major individuals associated with it. In doing this, we have attempted to present the unfoldment of vegetarianism chronologically, integrating both East and West in historical sequence, but maintaining each in separate chapters pertaining to the particular time period involved.

In the contemporary world, the ancient vegetarian current of the classical Greco-Roman world merges with that of India and the Far East. To these are added the more recent vegetarian perspectives which developed chiefly in Britain and North America during the 19th and 20th centuries. All of these elements contribute to the essentially syncretistic vegetarianism of the contemporary world.

Vegetarianism is a "way of life" which has a very ancient pedigree going back into prehistory. In whatever historical context, it has never been a phenomenon which is isolated from the other aspects of human life, culture, and concerns. Rather, it is something which is intimately bound up with philosophy, religion, and ethics; with custom and "taboo;" with attitudes towards Nature and the animal world; with aesthetics; with health and nutrition; and even with our particular theoretical beliefs and intuitive perceptions concerning history, time, and reality. For instance, the ancient idea of a "Golden Age" in man's primordial past, which was popular in ancient Greece and which came to the fore again during the Renaissance, is not without pertinence to the rebirth of vegetarianism in the West.

Generally, the development of vegetarianism in a specific culture has gone hand in hand with other social, ethical, and religious issues. Thus, in both ancient India and ancient Greece, opposition to animal sacrifice was closely linked to the advocacy of a vegetarian diet. In Victorian and pre-Victorian England, vegetarianism or "humane diet"—although seeded by both the Greco-Roman Revival and increased British contact with the culture and thought of India and the East—to a large degree developed *as one aspect* of a much broader programme of progressive Humanist social reform.

Despite the length of this book, it provides little more than an outline of the history of vegetarianism, relating this subject in its various stages of development to the particular historical milleu. Each section could be expanded into a study in itself. Indeed, it is to be hoped that many of the topics, ideas, and individuals only briefly touched upon here in this outline history of vegetarianism may suggest to readers subjects for further development and investigation in studies both academic and otherwise. At any rate, for the present time, this volume at least provides a relatively brief presentation of the essentials of vegetarian history from a strictly vegetarian perspective.

Vegetarianism and its place in human life as a viable dietary alternative is something extremely pertinent to the world today when there is a greatly increased sense of "healing the earth," which is to say, restoring it to its natural wholeness. If there is one phenomenon that is of basic importance in "healing the earth," it is to treat animal beings with respect, empathy, and compassion—and consequently to observe a strictly vegetarian diet.

To kill and eat harmless animal beings is to fragment reality and sunder the wholeness of being. To heal the earth is to not only refrain from all acts which harm other beings, both human and non-human, but to actively manifest kindliness, compassion, and understanding towards all beings according to one's capacities. It is to such an end of restoring the natural wholeness of life that this study is dedicated.

1. The "Golden Age" — Legendary Beginnings

Long before the beginnings of recorded history, hidden deep within the mists of the past in an ancient primordial world, there existed, according to indelible memory imprints preserved in the consciousness of mankind, a time known as the "Golden Age."

We need not concern ourselves with the many obscure legends which exist concerning the "Golden Age." What interests us here are only those aspects of that age which are pertinent to the subject with which this study is concerned. Suffice it to say that the "Golden Age" was perceived as a time of harmony and non-violence; a time wherein animals were neither sacrificed on altars, hunted, nor eaten by man; a time of peace, abundant crops, and beneficent climate.

While the "Golden Age" may be understood as having existed in the remote past on this planet, or on some other world from which this world is derived, it may also be viewed as a present potentiality as well as a future certainty. In this respect, one may observe that most futuristic utopias, ranging from those of ancient Greece to those of the Renaissance, have featured in their projected societies, certain elements of the population who abstain from the flesh of animals. This fact would seem to indicate that deep within himself, man realizes that the killing and eating of animals is ethically unacceptable.

The most ancient literary source for the "Golden Age" is *Works and Days* by the 8th century B.C. poet and moralist, Hesiod, who may be cited as one of the earliest known western vegetarians. One may note, too, that an extremely archaic tradition of vegetarian observance prevailed among certain priestly orders in ancient Egypt,[1] although the practice of vegetarianism was by no means common in that land. Some 500 years after Hesiod, in the 3rd century B.C., Aristus also wrote of the "Golden Age" in his poem *Phaenomenae*.

It is not without interest that according to an ancient tradition that can be traced to Hesiod, the inhabitants of the "Golden Age" seek to become "daimons" or "guardian spirits" in future ages, encouraging such basic ethical observances as non-violence and the compassionate treatment of all sentient beings as well as the consequent maintenance of a vegetarian diet.

There was a general concensus among the ancient Greeks that the first or "Golden Age" was to be perceived as a reflexion of "heaven" or a higher "ideal world" wherein man was closer to the "Gods" or his "extra-terrestrial instructors." According to Crates, it was a "lost world" where man still possessed the ability to communicate with the animals. It was seen as an age when, in the words of Porphyry, "men sacrificed to the Gods, fruits and not animals."[2] "No altar then was wet with the blood of bulls irrationally slain," continues Porphyry. Indeed, he states that "this (that is, animal sacrifice) was thought to be of every impious deed, the worst."[3] "One may note that even in Porphyry's own day (the 3rd century A.D.), the ancient practice of the "Golden Age" continued, as it had from the beginning of time, uninterrupted at the altar of Apollo in Delos, on which no animal had ever been allowed to be sacrificed.

In the periods following the "Golden Age," a gradual degeneration or "devolution" was believed to have taken place in successive "metalic" ages, finally culminating in violence, disharmony, wars between men, and the killing and eating of animals. Yet, the whole process was seen within a broader perspective of "recurring" historical cycles and an optimistic belief in the possibility of an eventual "recovery" of the past—a "recovery" of what had been and the eventual coming into existence of a "New Age" which, in fact, involved a return to the primordial past with its higher ethics and its greater sensitivity towards Nature and the animal world.

It is not our concern here to separate fact from legend and mythical accretions in regard to the "Golden Age" and the possibility of its conjunction with some now-lost "high civilization" and ethic. What is important is that man, at a very early period of history believed that such an "Age" had existed and that in it, animals were neither killed nor eaten.

2. *The Foundations of Western Vegetarianism— Pythagoras and His Teachings*

c. 550-500 B.C.

Despite man's almost universal memory of vegetarianism as prevailing in the "Golden Age" of a remote primordial past, it would seem that aside from certain worshippers of Orpheus and Apollo as well as occasional individual practitioners, vegetarianism had all but disappeared by the 6th century B.C.

In the first half of the 6th century B.C., there appeared in Greece one of the most notable individuals in the history of mankind. The name of this great man was Pythagoras (582-500 B.C.), and he was born on the island of Samos off the coast of Asia Minor. Most of what we know concerning Pythagoras, who may be aptly termed "the father of western vegetarianism," derives from biographies which were written many centuries after Pythagoras's lifetime. These include those by Apollonius of Tyana, Porphyry, Iamblicus, Diogenes Laertius, and others. Such biographies were based on surviving oral traditions which were often quite contradictory and in certain cases not at all reliable. Nevertheless, once one has separated the chaff from the wheat and has rejected certain elements as impossibly irrational or even slanderous, many essential facts emerge from these diverse sources.

Viewed as a vehicle of religious revelation, as a "messenger" from another world or even as an ephiphany of Apollo by many of his followers, Pythagoras incorporated in himself not only the ethical and spiritual leader, but the scholar and scientist as well. Remembered today almost exclusively for his mathematical learning and his creative innovations in that area of human intellectual endeavour, the fact is that Pythagoras was, in his own day and 1ong after, known no less for the profundity of his astronomical and medical knowledge as well as for the elaborate system of musical theory which he preserved and developed. What is more, he was seen as a great philosopher and teacher of ethics as well as something of a "magus"—one who could draw on unseen powers and forces in the manifestation of extraordinary mental, physical, and psychical feats.

After extensive travels among both the Babylonians and Egyptians, Pythagoras migrated to the city of Croton or Cretona on the southern tip of the Italian Peninsula, then part of Magna Graecia or "Greater Greece" and the centre of the Greek colony in Italy. Known as a medical and athletic centre, Croton was a port city of some 12 miles in circumference and was famous for its shrine to Hercules. There, in Croton, Pythagoras founded his spiritual-philosophic-scientific academy, to which, incidently, women were admitted on an equal standing with men. Gradually, the Pythagorean Academy became an extremely influential institution which, as a centre of ethics and learning as well as the preserver of a higher and very ancient knowledge, eventually became the governing body of the city of Croton.

Pythagoras was an individual with a strong sense of "mission" and was very much of a "reformer"—of both ethics and of the conventional religious rites and beliefs which prevailed in the Greece of his day. It is within this context that his advocacy of vegetarianism should be seen. As a religious reformer, he strongly objected to animal sacrifice in the temples and on Mount Olympus where scores of oxen were sacrificed to Zeus. He believed that such rites of blood sacrifice were not only unethical, inasmuch as they involved the suffering and killing of animal beings which man had a moral obligation to treat in a kindly fashion, but were also demeaning of the Numinous Forces which the Gods were held to represent! In his view, blood sacrifice was not only barbaric and unethical, but supremely irrational.

What is more, he condemned not only the sacrificial killing of animals and the very concept of the efficacy of "blood sacrifice," but also the eating of the flesh of the sacrificed animals by priests and worshippers alike. In this regard, one may observe that such a custom, "sanctified" by the religious context in which it occurred could only lead to a total insensitivity of the participants to animals on a secular level within the ordinary circumstances of everyday life. In other words, blood sacrifice in the temples set a bad example for society as a whole. Thus, Pythagoras made it his mission to not only oppose—through appeals to ethic and to reason—blood sacrifice and the consumption of such sacrificed animals in the temples, but the killing and eating of all animals, including fish, everywhere, at all times, and in all possible circumstances!

According to tradition, Pythagoras believed in the "blood brotherhood" of men and beasts. Indeed, it is said that he was sensitive even to the suffering of fish and that not infrequently he would walk down to the sea, purchase whole nets-full of suffocating fish from the fishermen and return them to their natural element, the life-giving ocean. Similarly, he took great pleasure in buying and then freeing caged birds destined for the table.

The teachings of Pythagoras involved not only a rejection of "blood sacrifice" to the gods, but also an affirmation of man's ethical obligation to treat animals with kindness and compassion. From the Pythagorean perspective, the killing (and, hence the eating) of animal beings is indicative of a "de-rangement" or "dis-memberment" of that natural wholeness and harmony of Being which is the essence of existence itself.

Pythagorean ethic and practice involved becoming "attuned" to the underlying harmony of Being, the natural "harmony of the spheres." This "attunement" was seen as involving an integrated synthesis of astronomical, musical, medical, and mathematical knowledge. It was also experienced in terms of existing in perfect harmony with the animal world. Our natural kinship with other animal life forms should automatically rule out the killing and eating of them as a violation of cosmic integrity. Instead, man should seek to develop an intuitive communication with the animals through cultivating a sensitive empathy with them. Pythagoras himself, through both empathetic kindness and through utilizing the "magical" lure of musical sound, enjoyed a perfectly harmonious relationship with the animal world. He is even said to have been able to stroke the backs of wild eagles and to have tamed a savage predatory bear.

The specific way of life which Pythagoras sought to implement among his followers involved not only the abandonment of animal sacrifice and the eating of animals, but also a deep immersion in the sciences of mathematics, astronomy, and music as well as diverse meditations, some of which involved breathing exercises intended to evoke memory residues or traces from "past lives" and create a harmonious "placement'" of the individual within the particular circumstances of his immediate existence. Indeed, it was said of him that "he knew who he was himself and who he had been."[4]

Although the idea of "re-incarnation" played a part in Pythagorean teachings, we will not concern ourselves here with the particular theories of "transmigration" to which Pythagoras subscribed or how he understood or interpreted this phenomenon.

Let it suffice to say that "memory exercises" concerned with the "re-collection" of multiple memories (as in recalling incidents from the lives of the dead as via the remaining residues or traces of their consciousness) were of major importance in the Pythagorean discipline, such knowledge being seen as enabling the practitioner to escape the otherwise inevitable cycle of death and rebirth. "Recollection" and "memory" were viewed as the basis of knowledge or wisdom which had been gradually accumulated in numerous "past lives."

The aim of Pythagorean practice was said to have been "the falling into place," as in a pattern, of memory fragments through their "re-collection" which resulted in a "correct" working out of individual destiny. Included in this whole discipline was the idea that man had access to memory fragments deriving from the "other worlds" of his primordial origins and that these "memory fragments" and the theories and legends which evolved out of them contained important clues as to the "nature of things," while at the same time veiling Reality at its deepest level.

For man to return to his Numinous or Divine source of being, Pythagorean ethic held that he must refrain from all forms of violence and never be the cause of suffering in other beings. Hence, the Pythagorean opposition to war, hunting, and the killing of animals for food, sacrifice, or any other reason. Such phenomena were all seen as involving a "de-rangement" and "dis-memberment" of reality, as a fragmentation of the natural wholeness and harmony of Being.

The Pythagorean goal was a "return" to the mental-psychical-physical health and harmony of the "Golden Age," the primordial past wherein a superior ethic prevailed and men lived in peace with one another and with the animals, neither hurting nor eating the latter. The adoption of a vegetarian diet was seen as a basic step in the purification of a barbaric, "de-volved" world—all to the end of its transformation and "return" to the "high civilization," sensitivity, and ethic of the distant past.

Man was, in fact, seen by Pythagoras and his followers as "an exile from another world"—thus perhaps indicating not only the world of the "Golden Age," but hinting at a world behind and beyond the ancient "Golden Age." For some persons, of the contemporary world at least, this suggests other-planetary origins amidst the stars and a civilization from beyond the earth.

The cult of Apollo at Delos became particularly associated with Pythagoras and his followers. Delos is a small island in the centre of the Cyclades. It was sacred to Apollo whose festivities were celebrated with song, dance, and athletic contests. It was also a centre of the grain trade as well as a place where banking and treasury activities were concentrated. There, at the shrine of Apollo, as a survival of "Golden Age" practice, the offerings to the God had always remained strictly limited to grains, fruits, and vegetables. There, no vultures circled above blood-spattered altars and the pathetic corpses of sacrificed animals. Rather, Helios the sun, symbol of Apollo, shone down on the "first fruits" of the good earth in a kind of perpetual "harvest festival," recalling to mankind the bounteous qualities of Nature and the joys of a healthful and ethical vegetarian diet. Hence, states Porphyry, "the Pythagoreans having adopted this mode of sacrifice, abstained from animal food through the whole of life."[5]

Ovid in his *Metamorphosis* states that Pythagoras expressed himself in words such as the following: "The earth affords a lavish supply of riches, of innocent foods that involve no bloodshed or slaughter . . . We have grain . . . and grapes swelling on the vines. There are herbs and vegetables . . . Nor are you denied milk or honey."[6] Pita bread, olives, cooked wheat and barley, millet, oil, milk, honey, raw and cooked fruits and vegetables, particularly cabbage and figs are said to have comprised the basic items of the Pythagorean diet.

As for Pythagoras's ban on the eating of beans, a ban which has caused considerable puzzlement in some circles and led to mockery of the "Pythagorean diet" in others, this proscription is solidly based on a very real danger—namely, the development of a disease termed "favism." To begin with, it may be noted that the only type of bean known in the Mediterranean regions during the time of Pythagoras and long after was *the fava bean*. The condition known as "favism" is caused by the consumption of fava beans. According to medical science, it is an hereditary condition which is the result of allergic reaction to this species of bean—a reaction which causes the development of "hemolytic anemia." It is said to effect only Mediterranean peoples, particularly Greeks and Italians, *and only a very small number of them.* That this disease may have been particularly prevalent in the area around Croton, fully justifies Pythagoras's ban at the time. The disease is said to be a rarity today.

Interestingly enough, Pythagoras wrote an entire treatise on the healing powers of cabbage which he recommended in the treatment of both internal and external disorders. This work is no longer extant, but it reveals that from its very beginnings, western vegetarianism has been concerned with matters of health and disease prevention as well as ethics.

Pythagoras also saw the immense importance of music to human health, both physical and mental. For the Pythagoreans, the desired state of health and harmonious being required not only a "pain-free diet," which is to say strictly vegetarian food which has not involved the suffering and death of any animal beings, but also a "tuning in" to "the music of the spheres." This was perceived in terms of an underlying cosmic harmony of being, manifest in certain musical notes and sounds in which opposites were balanced in conjunction with a system of correspondences between these sounds and notes on one hand and certain celestial configurations of sun, moon, stars, and planets on the other. These celestial bodies were, in turn, identified with certain numbers. Thus, for the Pythagorean, musical notes or sounds, precisely arranged according to both mathematical and astronomical correspondences, took on a kind of quasi-"magical" quality which was seen as leading to a "transformation" of the hearer through auditory participation in the essential cosmic harmony.

From such a perspective, music itself becomes not only a "healing medicine," but also a kind of auditory "sacrament" through which both physical and spiritual health are maintained. Through manifesting "the harmony of the spheres" and of the cosmos itself, music (which is to say music composed according to Pythagorean musical theory) purifies the psyche of the hearer, not only providing him with an emotional stability and a cosmically-grounded tranquility, but also evoking a clarity of mind and perception.

Unfortunately, over the years, a certain hostility built up against Pythagoras and his "initiates." The reasons for this were varied. First and foremost was the fact that the Pythagorean communities had spread throughout much of Hellenic Italy, forming a kind of esoteric "network." Furthermore, in many areas, they had assumed a certain degree of political power which—considering the fact that the Pythagorean initiates represented an unquestionably superior wisdom and ethic dating to a remote past—is hardly surprising. Their esoteric "elitism" with its innermost core of secret teachings and its goal of theosis or "deification" did not, it would seem, endear Pythagoreanism to the general public, which resented both its unconventional perspectives and its opposition to many established customs. One might have expected that its advocacy of a vegetarian diet would have been a thoroughly acceptable phenomenon in the heavily agricultural society of the time. Yet, this, too, became a matter of considerable contention on the part of the common people. The established priesthood was also quick to take advantage of the situation, encouraging the populace to oppose the "heterodoxy" of Pythagoras who not only promoted the observance of a vegetarian diet, but was opposed to animal sacrifice in the temples as well.

In any case, as general hostility towards the Pythagorean adepts increased, attacks against them became more and more frequent. Eventually, most of their buildings were destroyed and the majority of Pythagorean adepts massacred by mobs of ruffians at the behest of one Cylon, a wealthy landowner who, for reasons of his own and encouraged by the orthodox pagan priesthood, hated Pythagoras and his teachings with a vengeance, viewing Pythagoreanism as a serious threat to the conventional mores, customs, and society of the day. Thus, Pythagoreanism was suppressed in the land where it had arisen—Hellenic Italy.

Some Pythagorean initiates, however, escaped to Greece proper. Among them were Lysis and Philolaus of Thebes, both of whom, during the 5th century B.C., established centres of Pythagorean teaching at Philius and Thebes in Greece. Thus, Pythagorean wisdom in its various forms continued to exist and be propagated. Somewhat later, Philolaus returned to Hellenic Italy and re-established Pythagoreanism at Tarentum.

By the 4th century, however, serious divergences began to appear among those claiming to be adherents of Pythagoras and his teachings. Numerous "sub-schools," sects, and "sections" came into existence. In other words, a fragmentation occurred. While some were interested only in mathematics, astronomy, or musical theory, others confined themselves to the ethical, spiritual, and psychical aspects of Pythagoreanism. What is more, diverse interpretations and different schools arose. As a result, endless confusion has ensued. To add to this, the opponents of Pythagoreanism in any and all of its many diverse aspects (except Pythagorean mathematical science which alone became accepted as a "respectable" element of human learning) busied themselves in endless slanders concerning Pythagoras and his teachings. Such detractors not infrequently secured the services of both comic "poets" and low-level street-theatre performers who indulged themselves in various defamations, distortions, and scurrillous tales concerning the great apostle of vegetarianism in the West.

3. Vegetarian Foundations in the East—The Hindu and Jain Background

c. 600–500 B.C.

Just as ancient Greece is quite clearly the source of vegetarianism in the West, India is unquestionably the fount of vegetarianism in the East. Prior to discussing our subject within its Jain and Buddhist contexts, it is expedient to summarize briefly the circumstances and extent to which vegetarianism was (and is) a required observance in Hinduism.

In the 6th century B.C., only members of the brahman caste, religious ascetics, and the monks and devotees of certain specific sects within Hinduism were truly vegetarian. *All* Hindus, however, did abstain from the eating of cows, calves, bulls, and oxen. These animals were, in fact, seen as "sacred," inasmuch as milk and the resulting dairy products were derived from the species. This abstention from the killing and eating of kine was observed chiefly as a "taboo," although the extremely devout sometimes saw beyond the taboo to the ethical basis of the observance, and, to be sure, many persons felt a genuine sense of gratitude to the species for the nourishing milk products which formed such an important part of the Indian diet.

While the followers of certain specific cults within Hinduism—such as Vishnuites, for whom fish is forbidden—abstained from other species of animals as well, the majority of Hindus had no compunction whatever about killing and eating various animals ranging from chickens to goats and sheep. What is more, blood or animal sacrifice was widely practiced according to ancient Vedic rites in temples throughout India—particularly in the worship of Shiva, Kali, and Durga.

THE JAINS

Jainism is sometimes termed the "pre-Vedic religion of India." Very different from Hinduism, Jainism in its present form dates to the great Mahavira who lived during the 6th century B.C. In this ancient religion, a respect for animal life and the observance of a strictly vegetarian diet constitute ethical absolutes which are incumbant upon each and every person who accepts the Jain Path as a way of life.

Inasmuch as it rejects any notion of a creator god as well as any idea of "divine grace" as both irrational and unethical, particularly in view of the relevance of karma to individual human destinies, Jainism may be viewed as essentially atheistic. Consequently, the Jain emphasis is on self-effort and individual initiative in the attainment of good karma and the liberation from karmic bondage or "samsara." Basic to Jain ethic is the commission of good deeds and carrying out in one's life the principle of Ahimsa towards all beings, both human and animal.

Ahimsa first and foremost involves non-harming and non-violence. Human behaviour which violates this ethical principle—as in wars of aggression, hunting, fishing, or in any way harming or being neglectful of animal life—is very strictly proscribed. Such conduct is seen as not only morally bad in itself, but is viewed in terms of the negative karma which it accrues to the doer.

The "Holy Ones" or Saints of the Jain religion who receive the veneration of Jain believers are termed "Tirthankaras" or "Ford-makers over the ocean of existence." Such individuals are seen as beings who have attained final release from karmic bondage and reached the end of their journey through, what is sometimes termed "the cycle of destinies." The most recent and most revered of Jain Tirthankaras or "Saint-Teachers" is the great Mahavira (599-527 B.C.). Mahavira initiated various reforms and energetically propagated the ethics of an absolute Ahimsa throughout much of India, winning many converts from among the Hindus and absorbing within Jainism a religious order dedicated to the non-injury of sentient beings and founded some 250 years before by the monk, Parshva.

Although the Jainism of Mahavira's time was decidedly monastic in outlook and hence notably ascetic in orientation, today the majority of Jains are lay-people or "householders," many of whom are merchants.

The first vow or "vrata" taken by the Jain believer is one which asserts "the inviolability of life." This is understood as involving the principle: "Neither kill nor cause to kill," and is seen as proscribing the eating of meat no less than actually killing an animal or hiring an assassin! Likewise, the core of Jain teaching is revealed in the following verses of the *Dasavaitalika Sutra*—"Knowledge leads to compassion; compassion is manifest in behaviour. *Whatever beings are, whether moving or non-moving, thou shall not hurt . . .* All beings love life . . . Therefore, a nirgantha (disciple or person on the path) refrains from all acts of injury."[7]

The Jain goal is to make the principle of Ahimsa permeate the whole of life and society. This involves not only maintaining a strictly vegetarian diet, but also treating all beings with empathy and kindness. Thus, Jainism has always opposed caste restrictions, meaningless taboos, and inequalities. Mahavira, for instance, made a point of welcoming persons of all castes, including the so-called "untouchables," to the Jain religion. This, as much as Mahavira's vehement opposition to animal sacrifice, was the cause of extreme hostility and even persecution of the Jains on the part of orthodox Hinduism, particularly those sects of the latter which made animal sacrifice a pivotal point of religious practice.

Not without interest is the fact that both Mahavira's (599-527 B.C.) and Pythagoras's (582-500 B.C.) opposition to animal sacrifice coincided in time. In each case, too, these two great spiritual leaders and apostles of the vegetarian way of life found themselves faced with considerable opposition on the part of the orthodox priesthoods of their respective lands.

In some ways, Jain vegetarianism is hardly representative of vegetarianism in general. Jains, for instance, differ from other vegetarians in that they do not eat "root vegetables" such as turnips, beets, carrots, or celeriac—all of which are extremely important in the diets of most other vegetarians throughout the world. It may be observed, too, that they differ from Hindu and perhaps the majority of modern vegetarians in their abstinence from all dairy products. In this, however, they are one with those contemporary western vegetarians who term themselves "vegans."

In conclusion, it may be noted that the influence of Jainism in the historical development of vegetarianism cannot be over-estimated. This is made abundantly clear in the little-publicized fact that the Jain doctrine of Ahimsa or "non-harming" as an absolute pivot of human ethics is the same as that propagated even in this century by Mahatma Gandhi who acknowledged that he derived it from the Jain religion and who spoke of being profoundly influenced by his contemporary, Jain layperson, Raychandbhai Mehta.

4. Vegetarian Observance in Buddhism— An Indisputable Fact

C. 530 B.C.–1ST CENTURY A.D.

Just as the spread of Jainism through the energetic missionary endeavours of Mahavira gave considerable impetus to the growth of vegetarianism in India during the 6th century B.C., so did the appearance of the Gautama Buddha, Shakyamuni (563-483 B.C.) who, in fact, is said to have spent some time as a Jain ascetic.

Like Jainism, Buddhism firmly opposed many aspects of the Hindu establishment—ranging from its caste system to the dreadful animal sacrifices of the old Vedic rituals and the fundamentalist literalism with which Hinduism viewed the gods of its pantheon.

That Buddhism, from its inception, enjoined treating all animals with kindness and compassion as well as required the observance of a vegetarian diet cannot be denied. The first or basic precept of Buddhism, that of Ahimsa or Non-harming, decisively prohibits the killing and infliction of suffering on sentient beings, whether men or animals. Needless to say, this precept cannot be reconciled with the eating of animal flesh any more than it can with hunting, fishing, or the butchering of animals! From the Buddhist perspective, the killing and eating of animals not only violates Buddhism's basic ethical principle of Ahimsa, but also creates a negative psychic atmosphere and perpetuates karmic bondage.

Many Buddhist *Sutras*, sacred texts, hagiographies, and moral admonitions leave no doubt whatever concerning vegetarianism as an ethical requirement for all who follow the Buddhist spiritual path, very clearly condemning the eating of animals while commending and explicitly requiring a strictly vegetarian diet for all "practitioners of the Dharma," both lay persons and monks. Indeed, it was only many centuries after the foundation of Buddhism that

Buddhist practice in this respect came to differ from country to country and school to school.

The *Lankavatara*, a *Sutra* which is termed "the essence of the Teaching of all the Buddhas," is a primary source of ethical injunctions strictly prohibiting the consumption of animal flesh by all persons claiming to follow the Path of the Buddha. The reader is urged to see the D. T. Suzuki translation of this *Sutra*, Sutra Section 244-259, pages 211-222, published by Kegan Paul Ltd., London, 1956.

In the *Lankavatara*, the "no meat" injunction is unconditional, and mendicant or begging monks are not cited as "exempt" out of ascetic disregard for what they consume as they sometimes are in other sources. Likewise, the idea, common among Theravadin Buddhists today, that meat is permitted to followers of the Buddha provided that they did not kill the animal themselves is explicitly condemned. The compassionate heart, states this *Sutra*, cannot be reconciled with the eating of tortured and murdered animals. Such are referred to by the *Sutra* as "unnatural food."[8] All members of the Dharma are, in fact, advised to view all animal beings as no different than their own children, and hence to be treated with the same kindness, solicitude, and concern for their well-being. "Wherever there is the evolution of living beings," states the Tathagata, "let people cherish a sense of kinship with them, and thinking that all beings are to be loved as if they were an only child, let them refrain from eating meat."[9]

"Nowhere in the *Sutras*," admonishes the *Lankavatara*, is meat permitted . . . nor is it referred to as proper among the foods prescribed for the Buddha's followers."[10] Even in "exceptional cases" or as "skillful means"—such as eating meat in order "to be polite" or in order to gain a person's confidence for the purpose of leading them to eventual enlightenment—the consumption of meat is proscribed. Indeed, the Buddha is quoted as stating unequivocally: "Meat eating is forbidden by me everywhere and for all time for all who are abiding in compassion."[11]

Interestingly enough, the reasons given for the prohibition of meat eating in the *Lankavatara* include not only the basic ethical imperative of not harming sentient beings (that of the compassionate heart), but the simple fact of man's kinship with the rest of the animal world. Hence, the injunction to regard each animal as one's own child. Also noting that meat is "repulsive" and has "a nauseating odour," the *Sutra* observes that eating meat "stupifies the mind" as well as involves one in the "habit-energy of evil karma."[12]

Rather curiously, neither nutrition nor disease prevention are mentioned as reasons for maintaining a vegetarian diet, although certain specific foods are recommended by the *Sutra*—namely lentils, beans, rice, barley, clarified butter, honey, and sugar cane.[13] One might observe here, too, that traditionally, from very early times, tea has been very much part of the Buddhist diet.

Other *Sutras*, besides the *Lankavatara*, which explicitly condemn the eating of meat in all circumstances include the *Anglimalika, Mahaparinirvana, Mahamega, Hastikakshaya*, and the *Surangama*. The latter, for instance, states that no one who does not find unkindness and killing—and by extension, meat-eating—totally abhorrent can escape from karmic bondage. It also warns that there will come a time when "different kinds of ghosts" (evil spirits) will be encountered everywhere, deceiving people and teaching them that they can eat meat and still obtain enlightenment.[14]

ASOKA

Definitive evidence as to the extent to which early Buddhism encouraged and indeed prescribed the observance of vegetarianism may be seen in the life and edicts of the great Emperor of India, Asoka—termed more formally, Asokavardhana—who reigned from 274 to 232 B.C. His symbol was the peacock, this being the meaning of his family name, Moriya (sometimes rendered by the alternative spelling "Mauriya").

Asoka inherited a vast empire from his father and exchanged embassies even with several Greek kingdoms in the West. In his Hindu youth, Asoka was noted as a ferocious warrior and cruelly cunning hunter. Upon his conversion to Buddhism, he recoiled in revulsion from both war and hunting, never engaging in these activities again. Indeed, his former hunting expeditions were replaced by visits to Buddhist holy men and pilgrimages to Buddhist holy sites. What is more; he took it upon himself to alleviate human and animal suffering in every way possible.

During his long reign, Asoka became an ideal ruler, embodying in himself the Buddhist ethical ideal of compassionate action in numerous ways. Everywhere, he ordered the setting up of "pillars of life" on which were inscribed Buddhist precepts for "right living." In these, he particularly emphasized Ahimsa and the sanctity of life, both human and animal. Imploring his subjects to treat all sentient beings with kindness and compassion and to cease being the cause of any form of suffering, Asoka set a many-faceted example for them to follow by building hospitals for people and for animals as well as providing free medicines and treatment for all in need. He also built hostels and had watering places created throughout the country.

Not only did Asoka adopt a strictly vegetarian diet himself, but he encouraged his subjects to do the same. In his Rock Edict #1, he also forbade the barbaric practice of animal sacrifice on the part of the orthodox Hindu priesthood. This edict, of course, resulted in considerable enmity towards him on the part of the Hindus, whom he had already alienated through his conversion to Buddhism. Actually, Asoka himself was extremely tolerant of other religions and schools of thought. One of his Rock Edicts even forbade the disparagement of religions in general, but he demanded that his subjects refrain from harming animals. As for hunting, he made it strictly illegal early in his reign.

Although Buddhism continued to exist for many centuries in India after the death of the great emperor, Asoka, it ceased to retain the privileged status which it possessed under his patronage. With Hindu rulers again in control, the brahman priesthood strove to oppose the spiritual perspectives of Buddhism, which were radically different from its own in every way possible. Ultimately, in order to draw Buddhists back into the Hindu cult as well as to deprive Buddhism of any influence in Indian life and culture as a separate religion, the Buddha was absorbed into the Hindu pantheon as a minor incarnation of Vishnu.

While the vegetarian practice inherent in original Buddhist teaching was clearly and unequivocally manifest in numerous sutras and in the universal Buddhist practice which prevailed during the 40-year reign of Asoka as well as in Chinese Buddhism from its inception in the 1st century A.D. to the present,* such was not the case with the Buddhism of southeast Asia. There, in the lands today comprising Burma, Thailand, Cambodia, and Vietnam, the original Buddhist vegetarian ethic eventu-

---

* See Chapter 7 and Chapter 11 for the Buddhist vegetarian tradition in China.

ally became relegated to oblivion. Indeed, it seems to have been replaced with a mis-interpreted ideal of "non-attachment" which obligated both monks and lay people to be totally indifferent to the food which they consumed, even to the point of eating animal flesh without scruple! In short, in the Theravadin Buddhism of southeast Asia, the essential Buddhist sense of man's moral obligation to the animal world as a natural extension of the central core of Buddhist teaching—*compassion as an ethical absolute*—was sacrificed to the totally "a-ethical" ideal of "non-attachment" and not causing offense (as in refusing to eat whatever one is offered). In such a viewpoint, man's ethical obligation to treat all sentient beings with kindness and compassion—and hence to observe a strictly vegetarian diet— vanishes into nothingness. Such a point of view is, of course, dia- metrically opposed not only to the Mahayanist Bodhisattva Ideal, but to the vegetarian observance of early Buddhism.

As Zen roshi, Philip Kapleau points out (see his *Cherish All Life*), any attempt by Theravadins and others to attribute to the Bud- dha himself, words permitting the consumption of meat involve a blatant falsification and corruption of sacred texts! In other words, those passages in the Pali suttas which allow the eating of animal flesh (providing that the eater did not kill the animal himself or that it was not killed specifically for him) can only be regarded as self- indulgent sophistries or inventions to justify the unseemly passion of the writers for the consumption of animal flesh.

Here, one may observe that it cannot be too strongly empha- sized that in evaluating contradictory or divergent views expressed in certain Buddhist texts and scriptures, only those can be accepted as genuine which are both logically and heart-wise in accord with the Buddha's basic precept of Ahimsa or Non-harming and its manifestation in compassionate action. Those which are not, must be rejected as interpolations and falsifications. Thus, those Pali scriptures which contain statements permitting the consumption of animal flesh are to be viewed as having been deliberately altered!

5. Vegetarian Continuations in the Hellenic West— Post-Pythagoras

C. 480–20 B.C.

To return to vegetarianism in the West—which at that time was limited to Greece and its colonies in southern Italy—it may be observed that the great persecution of Pythagoras and his followers initiated by Cylon, by no means brought an end to the Pythagorean ethic and philosophy or to their manifestation in the observance of a vegetarian diet. Likewise, the various branches of Pythagorean learning continued to exist. What did disappear were the openly Pythagorean communities in which the various branches of Pythagorean scientific learning were integrated with the Pythagorean ethic and philosophy in a single whole. Clandestine Pythagorean communities, however, continued to exist behind the scenes. So too, various branches of Pythagorean scientific learning continued to exist openly, but as separate entities rather than as aspects of an integrated whole involving Pythagorean ethic and philosophy. There can be no question that the Pythagorean ethic and philosophy continued to exist among wide segments of the population, but on an individual rather than a communal or organized level. The imprint which Pythagoras left on Greek society of his time was a deep one which, for the next 500 or even 1,000 years was to inspire and sustain the existence of vegetarianism among a sizable minority of the population.

Many of the leading advocates of vegetarianism during this period were prominent in Greek intellectual, scientific, and literary life. Among these was Empedocles (495-435 B.C.), the great physician and philosopher of Hellenic Sicily who was born some 5 years after the death of Pythagoras. As an advocate of Pythagoras's teachings, he sought to carry on Pythagorean medical practice within the context of an integrated scientific system involving both musical theory and astronomy. As the pivot of this whole theory of health and treatment of disease, stood a strictly meat-free diet.

As a physician, Empedocles endorsed the vegetarian diet for reasons of nutrition, health, and disease-prevention. Secondly, he opposed the killing and eating of animals for ethical reasons, urging everyone to put an end to "the accursed slaughter."[15] Thirdly, he decried the consumption of animal flesh for aesthetic reasons as a loathsome and disgusting barbarity.

As for Plato (427-347 B.C.), he was influenced by the dedicated Pythagorean, Philolaus of Thebes, and unquestionably possessed considerable interest in Pythagoras. While apparently viewing vegetarianism as an ideal diet, particularly for philosophers, there is no evidence that he was a practicing vegetarian himself, although this actually *may have* been the case. He does, however, mention vegetarianism as one form of diet in *The Republic*, thus indicating the continued existence of the Pythagorean vegetarian ideals in his time (427-347 B.C.). Some, in fact, view Chapter 4 of Plato's *Republic* as a "veiled defence of vegetarianism."

The reader is urged to consult Dombrowski's *Philosophy of Vegetarianism* concerning the philosophies of Plato and Aristotle in relation to vegetarianism.[16] According to various traditions, Socrates is said to have been a vegetarian, although, as in the case of Plato, no evidence exists to support such a possibility.

It may be noted, too, that certain of the "Cynics," although vegetarianism was in no way part of their specific system of philosophy, nevertheless personally followed such a diet. For instance, Crates, a 4th century philosopher as well as his disciple Metrocles were both notably vegetarian in diet. While Crates made lentils his chief food, Metrocles lived primarily on lupin "beans" or rather seeds—a vegetable highly favoured in the ancient world.

Far more significant than the few Cynics who observed a vegetarian diet, was Theophrastes (372-287 B.C.). A strong advocate of vegetarianism as well as man's ethical obligations to the animal world, Theophrastes is remembered today chiefly for his botanical studies and classifications. In his day, he was noted no less as a moralist who viewed the killing and eating of animal beings as ethically unacceptable. Although Theophrastes had been a pupil of Aristotle, he firmly rejected the latter's decidedly negative and even derogatory views of animal being.

Aristotle was not, of course, alone in the ancient world in his denial of man's moral obligation to treat animals with compassion and consideration. Certain Stoics went still further, denying not only man's kinship with the animals, but their actual sentience! Indeed, such persons, even at that early date, utilized ridicule and "reductio ad absurdium" in their undisguised contempt for the entire vegetarian perspective and practice as well as for the animals themselves, not unlike the more "retarded" elements of western society in our present century. Yet, even a few Stoics themselves, such as Musonius and Epicetus (1st century A.D.)—Contrary to the majority of adherents of this school—did observe a vegetarian diet. This fact is indicative of the extent to which vegetarianism and anti-vegetarianism have often existed side by side on the part of different members within the same philosophical school or even the same religion.

6. The Great Pagan Vegetarian Revival in the Greco-Roman West—Ovid, Apollonius of Tyana, the Great Plutarch, Plotinus, Porphyry, and Others

C. 1ST CENTURY B.C.–6TH CENTURY A.D.

Although neither vegetarianism as a philosophical-ethical current nor followers of a strictly vegetarian diet were ever lacking in the ancient Greco-Roman world after the time of Pythagoras, there can be no doubt that vegetarianism as a major movement and way of life only re-asserted itself in the Greco-Roman world just before and during the first 500 years of the Christian era. This renaissance of the ancient Pythagorean diet and ethic was not, of course, thanks to any encouragement of vegetarianism on the part of Christianity. To the contrary, its inspirers and propagators were Pagans who, like Plutarch, either pointedly ignored Christianity, or were persons of a decidedly anti-Christian cast of mind. Such individuals held decidedly superior ethical values which were not only in opposition to those of Christianity, but to certain phenomena within the old Paganism as well—notably to animal sacrifice, haruspicia, and the ghastly cruelties of the amphitheatre which involved both men and beasts. The Pagan advocates of of the vegetarian way of life were proponents of a rationality and compassion which was traceable directly back to the great Pythagoras and which have been rare enough in any period of human history.

OVID

At the forefront of the Pagan Vegetarian Revival was Ovid or, to give his full name, Publius Ovidius Naso (43 B.C.-18 A.D.). An important literary figure of his day, Ovid was the preserver and popularizer for posterity of Classical Greco-Roman mythology as well as a notable poet of the erotic—a subject which held an endless fascination for him. He was also an advocate of the "Pythagorean diet," which is to say, vegetarianism.

In his *Metamorphosis*, Ovid depicted, as within an enormous tapestry, all the ancient Gods and great historical figures of the ancient world, elaborating the complicated archetypal story structures and plots which surrounded them. He was a superb, colourful, and intricately-detailed weaver of tales dating to man's ancient past.

As an advocate of a strictly vegetarian diet, Ovid in Book XV of the *Metamorphosis* utilizes the figure of Pythagoras to present such a point of view.* Although this aspect of him has been seldom emphasized, Ovid was actually very much of a "moralist." For him, ethic," above all, meant sensitivity to suffering—both animal and human. It also meant not to harm sentient beings in any way whatever. Hunters he condemns as "hurters," hunting being seen as essentially a criminal act. As for the sacrifice of animals to the Gods, he saw it as a "blasphemy" and "ruthless egoism," as an act which sought to implicate the Numinous Forces of Divinity themselves in human criminality!

He viewed the ingestion of animal flesh as both cannibalistic and unnatural; he believed that the man who slits the throat of a calf, hearing its anguished cry with deaf ears, might well be prone to murder a human being.[17] In other words, Ovid views the brutality and insensitive cruelty involved in the killing of animals as psychologically indicative of a potential for shedding human blood. He perceives the hurting and killing of animals in terms of a terrible deception and betrayal.

In highly emotional terms, he speaks of a sacrifical goat whose cry resembles that of a human infant. He mentions, too, the sorrowful sounds made by a cow witnessing a human butcher murdering her calf. Ovid's purpose is to incite man's natural but very much surpressed human sympathy and sensitivity concerning the suffering of sentient beings. Calling to mind the wealth of vegetables, fruits, grains, and herbs as well as milk products and honey which are

* See Ovid, *Metamorphosis*. Penguin Classics. London, 1970; Glenn, Edgar. *The Metamorphosis—Essays*. University Press of America. N.Y., 1986; and Galinsky, G. Karl. *Ovid's Metamorphosis*. University of California Press. Berkeley, 1975.

available to man—all foods which are free of bloodshed—Ovid, through the mouth of Pythagoras speaks of the sheer "wickedness" of eating the dead flesh of other sentient beings, *of feeding on death!*

Ovid praises the "Golden Age" of the past when there was neither treachery on the part of man nor fear of human treachery among the animals—a time of vegetarian plenty when humankind did not defile its lips with the blood and flesh of beasts and birds and fish; a time before human criminality emerged in the form of snares, nets, and barbed hooks! He particularly condemns the blatant ingratitude involved in killing sheep—animals who provide man with both wool for warmth and cheese for nourishment—as well as of oxen whose valuable toil in tilling fields should have rendered them especially dear to man. Here, it may be noted that Sara Mack's view (presented in her *Ovid.* Yale Univ. Press. New Haven, 1988) that Ovid's Pythagoras and his statements are what she terms "no more than a burlesque" must be firmly rejected. To the contrary, as both Glinsky and Dombrowsky point out (see bibliographic citations), it is precisely in Section XV of the *Metamorphoses* that Ovid is at his most serious, sincerely affirming his own vegetarian ethic via his portrayal of Pythagoras.

APOLLONIUS OF TYANA

Often overlooked as a prominent apostle of vegetarianism in the West during the Pagan Vegetarian Revival of the first century A.D. is Apollonius of Tyana (c. 4 B.C.-80 A.D.), whose life overlapped with the lives of Ovid and Plutarch. An Hellenic Neo-Pythagorean priest, philosopher, and missionary, Apollonius of Tyana was also a notable traveller who traversed enormous distances to visit both Persia and India. Nor were the closer lands of Egypt and Abyssinia unknown to him. In all of these places, he was received by kings and princes as well as high priests.

Most of what we know of Apollonius is derived from the biography of him written by Philostratus (172-245 A.D.). This book was based upon the notes of a disciple of Apollonius, one Damis the Syrian, and was compiled at the request of the remarkable philosophic Empress Julia Domna (d. 217 A.D.), the daughter of the Syrian high-priest Bassianus of Emesa and wife of the Emperor Septimus Severus (146-211 A.D.), a notable Hellenophil who in his later days utilized much of his time in scholarly studies of the great monuments and antiquities of Athens.

A patroness of the arts and of learning, Julia Domna was the centre of a literary-philosophical-artistic salon at the Imperial Court to which many sculptors, philosophers, religious leaders, antiquarians, and literary figures"—including Philostratus—were drawn. A follower of the Pythagorean current or school of the old Paganism herself, this remarkable woman possessed a broad span of knowledge encompassing many different aspects of human culture.

It was to popularize the basic Pythagorean doctrines of limiting rites of sacrifice strictly to fruits, vegetables, grains, and frankincense as well as to maintaining a strictly vegetarian diet that Julia Domna requested Philostratus to compile a life of Apollonius of Tyana who, about 100 years before, had sought to revive the ancient Pythagorean teachings. The interest on the part of both the Empress and Philostratus in Apollonius's attempt to bring about a revival of Pythagoreanism is indeed indicative of their own devotion to the vegetarian cause and their opposition to religious rites of "blood sacrifice."

Although the biography of Apollonius is generally viewed as semi-fictional, it nevertheless is of major importance as an indication of the continuing survival of the *genuine* Pythagorean tradition, both in terms of diet and of opposition to animal sacrifice during the final centuries of the old Greco-Roman religion and civilization.

As Philostratus states of him, Apollonius "would not stain the altar with blood; nay, rather the honey-cake and frankincense and hymns of praise were the offerings made to the Gods by this man."[18] Likewise, "he abstained from all flesh diet," both from sacrifices and for food. To the priests of Olympus, he wrote that the Gods were "in no need of sacrifices," by which he signified "blood sacrifices."[19] Apollonius also notes that certain "priests defile the altar with blood . . . and then people ask in amazement why our cities are visited with calamities."[20] "I have never sacrificed blood," he states emphatically. "This is the rule of Pythagoras and likewise of his disciples." Acceptable sacrifices or offerings to the Numinous, he advises, consist of "frankincense," "good actions," "honey cakes," and "first fruits."[21]

Apollonius views meat as "unclean," this quality deriving from the suffering that has been inflicted on the murdered animal as well as from the immorality of the act of shedding blood and depriving an animal being of life. He not only viewed the actual killer of the animal as guilty, but—by extension—the purveyors and eaters of the victim as well! Thus, like all genuine Pythagoreans, Apollonius ate only vegetables, grains, and fruits, seeing all of these as "clean."

During his extensive travels, Apollonius made a point of enlightening others in regard to the desirability of non-blood sacrifice in religious rites as well as the maintenance of a strictly vegetarian diet. In Egypt, for instance, he rebuked certain Egyptian priests for sacrificing bulls and birds, remarking that anyone who possessed even a little wisdom, would be capable of correcting their faulty rites.[22] Elsewhere, according to Philostratus, he boldly refused even kings to join with them in rites involving blood sacrifice, and, fortunately lived to tell the tale.

As a major reviver of Pythagorean ethic, Apollonius did not escape from being subjected to various forms of harassment and persecution. Variously accused of being a "wizard" and a "revolutionary" (inasmuch as he was partisan to Nerva, who was to become Emperor) as well as being subjected to many slanders of the vilest sort, Apollonius suffered numerous indignities and even imprisonment under Domition who—with the support of those who opposed the "Pythagorean diet" no less than those who were gauled by his opposition to blood sacrifice—was determined to destroy him. "Informers" appeared with monstrous accusations, spies and hirelings were suborned to submit false informations; from all directions came distortions of the great Neo-Pythagorean apostle's character and history. Many were the artifices, devices, and maneuverings utilized to destroy him. Totally irrelevant matters were introduced in order to conceal the truth and veil the persecution with a semblance of "legitimacy."

In the end, however, Apollonius triumphed over his persecuters. Not unimportant in this was the coming of Nerva to the imperial throne, this emperor being a follower of Pythagoras.

In concluding this section on Apollonius, it may be observed that he was not only a friend and protector of animals, a tireless advocate of both bloodless sacrifice and vegetarian diet, but was also a noted exorcist of "empusas" and "lamias" (certain evil spirits) in the healing of mental and physical illness. Apollonius, during his travels, was also much concerned with restoring tombs and offering libations for the dead.

As for Philostratus, upon the death of the Empress Julia, he left Rome and settled in Tyre where he completed various essays on Nature as well as on law. There, too, he wrote his *Gymnasticus*—a volume dedicated to the athletic games and the conduct and character of the participants. Although this book is no longer extant, one may be certain that in the advice which he set forth in it, Philostratus advocated a strictly vegetarian diet as of major importance not only to the health of the athletes, but to the formation of their character as well.

THE GREAT PLUTARCH

Perhaps the most important figure in the great Pagan Vegetarian Revival at the beginning of the Christian era was Plutarch (46 A.D.-120 A.D.), the great literary figure, historical biographer, moralist, and government administrator who had been a student of Posidonius. As a very high profile public figure, Plutarch set himself the task of promoting sensitivity and compassion on all levels through propagating the old Pythagorean ethic with its insistance on the observance of a vegetarian diet and its proscription of blood sacrifice in the temples. His times were not especially noted for gentleness. Indeed, his was an age when the gladitorial combats of the amphitheatre had to a considerable degree de-humanized and benumbed Roman society. Thus, one should by no means be suprised that such phenomena should evoke their opposite in the gentle Plutarch who sought not only to oppose brutality and barbarism, but to replace them with an ethics of kindliness and compassion.

Born and educated in Athens, Plutarch later settled in Rome where he became a major intellectual and ethical figure of his day. As Burrow points out,[23] Plutarch felt himself charged with a "mission" to preserve and make known the great achievements of the Hellenic past. A man of profound knowledge, Plutarch was, above all, a "transmitter" of ancient wisdom and ethic. Interestingly enough, he does not make a single reference to Christianity—then, still a very small sect—in any of his voluminous writings.

A leading scholar, historian, and biographer, Plutarch, like Pythagoras over 500 years before him, was also a priest of Apollo, whose ruined shrine at Delphi he spent considerable time and energy in restoring. There, he also served as "agonothetes" or director of the famous Pythian Games or athletic contests. As such, he also functioned as what in our own age would be termed a "chaplain" for the competing athletes to whom he unquestionably recommended a vegetarian diet as an ethical imperative as well as a benefaction to both their health and prowess.

As an individual whose encyclopedic knowledge of Classical Greco-Roman culture and history was perhaps more extensive than that of any other person of his era, Plutarch was appointed "instructor" to the Roman Emperor Hadrian, who later made the great man "Procurator of Greece," which by then had become a mere province of the Roman Empire.

Throughout much of his life, Plutarch was very much of a vegetarian "activist." As a leading intellectual and political figure, he took every opportunity to inculcate among the people of his day his own ethical and aesthetic revulsion towards the eating of animal beings.

Plutarch is noted for his *Lives* of the great as well as his *Table Talk* and many-volumed *Moralia*, which is a collection of essays. It is in Volume 12 of the *Moralia*[24] that his *On the Eating of Flesh* is found. In this essay, he appeals to all persons of compassionate humanity not to take the lives of animals, condemning as a "barbaric vice" the killing and eating of animal beings. Nor was his plea without effect. Many of the more cultured and educated Greeks and Romans of the day were moved by his advice to cease eating the flesh of animals and adopt a strictly vegetarian diet.

Plutarch exhorts all men to "excise" all "blood lust" from their lives in order to obtain "purity of soul." He views such pursuits as hunting or fishing as well as the professions of butchery and the raising of animals for table and the purveying of their mutilated corpses to the public as "evil ways of life."

The eating of animals is, for Plutarch, quite simply a form of cannibalism which has its roots in sadistic cruelty, in the frenzy of blood lust, and in unnatural insensitivity to other living beings who love their lives no less than we love ours. Addressing hunters, butchers, *and by extension*, meat-eaters, Plutarch asks: "What madness, what frenzy drives you to the pollution of shedding blood, you who have a superfluity of necessities? . . . Are you not ashamed to mingle domestic crops with blood and gore? You call . . . panthers and lions 'savage,' but you yourselves by your own foul slaughters leave them no room to outdo you . . . you slaughter harmless tame creatures without stings or teeth."[25]

Speaking of the animal-victims of man, he mentions the natural beauty and harmoniousness of their voices, their natural cleanliness, their keen intelligence, and their entitlement to live the full natural duration of their lives in peace and in natural enjoyment of the sun and of the earth without subjection to human cruelty and merciless exploitation. He speaks, too, of their "cries and entreaties for mercy" when faced with the human predator.[26] As for animal sacrifice in religious rites, he viewed it as essentially no different than human sacrifice, and condemns both as monstrous and barbaric evils.[27]

Plutarch specifically denies that the eating of animals is in any way "natural" to man. To the contrary, he emphasizes that man possesses neither the "hooked beak," nor the "sharp claws," nor the "jagged teeth" of the carnivore. Thus, he states, Nature itself "disavows our eating of flesh."[28] What is more, he believes that the killing and eating of animals is not only contrary to human nature, but that it makes man insensitive to all that is best and finest in his nature, causing him to become spiritually coarse as well as endangering his health.

Furthermore, Plutarch views the eating of animals as not only ethically unacceptable, but aesthetically repulsive as well. The "well-dressed" tables of the Roman gourmets of his day with their extensive displays of animal corpses (as indeed would be, say, the "Thanksgiving" and Christmas tables of non-vegetarians in North America today) were, for Plutarch, "ghastly grimoires" which should bring nausea, revulsion, and tears to the sensitive beholder. "What a terrible thing it is to look on when the tables . . . are spread by men who employ cooks and spicers to groom the dead . . . smothering with countless condiments the taste of the gore so that the palate may be deceived and accept what is foreign to it."[29] In essence, Plutarch's teaching may be reduced to the following words from his *Marcus Cato*: "Kindness and beneficence should be extended to creatures of every species."[30] Such a view quite clearly excludes even the remote possibility of observing any but a vegetarian diet.

PLOTINUS AND PORPHYRY

Although Porphyry is a figure of far greater importance in the history of vegetarianism than Plotinus, we mention the latter first here inasmuch as he came first chronologically and was the instructor of Porphyry who, as a vegetarian activist, became a leading figure of the great Pagan Vegetarian Revival.

Plotinus (204 A.D.-270 A.D.), Pagan moralist and spiritual leader, whose immediate teacher had been Ammonius Saccas, was born some 84 years after the death of Plutarch. He is known chiefly for his philosophical work *The Enneads*. Born in the then still-flourishing Hellenic city of Alexandria in northern Egypt where he received his education, Plotinus later journied to Rome where he was to spend the greater portion of his life propagating his philosophy which melded Neo-Platonic metaphysic with the doctrines and ethics of Pythagoras in an essentially "mystical" perspective involving "union with the One," the Numinous Energy or Force underlying all existence. In terms of external behaviour, a major aspect of ascent to "perfection" involved behaving in a kindly, benevolent, and compassionate manner towards *all* beings, both men and animals. Quite clearly, the natural consequences of such behaviour involved the maintenance of a vegetarian diet.

While references to vegetarianism as such are apparently lacking in the extant writings of Plotinus, that he strictly adhered to such a diet is attested by his disciple Porphyry, who writes in his *Life of Plotinus* that the great philosopher-mystic did "not approve of eating the flesh of animals," noting that he also refused to utilize any "medicines" derived from the bodies of animals (see Porphyry's *Life of Plotinus*[31] in the Loeb Edition of Plotinus's *Enneads*). That animals could be used for plowing and for wool, he viewed as perfectly acceptable as long as they were treated with kindness and consideration.

His concern was not so much with "theology" or the "nature of the Divine" as with "theurgy" or the experience of "oneness" with "the Numinous core of being"—as well as with the means attaining it. Treating men and animals with every possible kindness and the consequent observance of a strictly vegetarian diet were viewed as among those actions necessary in attaining "union with the Divine." For him, as for Pythagoras, mysticism and philosophy went hand in hand not only with an active ethics of compassion, but also with music and musical theory as well as with mathematics.

Porphyry (232 A.D.-305 A.D.), a leader of the Pagan Vegetarian Revival of his times, was a Phoenician Greek who received his education in Alexandria. Later, he traveled to Rome where he was to spend most of his life as a noted opponent of Christianity and an advocate of all that was best within the ancient Greco-Roman Paganism. He also spent much time in Sicily, an area with deep Pythagorean associations. Indeed, Pythagorean traditions, including the observance of a vegetarian diet, are said to have remained particularly strong there, and many of the inhabitants believed that Porphyry was guided by the very spirit of Pythagoras.

Interestingly enough, the great Pagan Vegetarian Revival with its attendant revitalization of Pagan ethic and philosophy, occurred within the context of a dying ancient world wherein the Christian Church was slowly increasing its hold on the minds and souls of Mediterranean man. Indeed, the resurgence of the Ancient Pagan Path of "Ascent to the Stars," as termed by the Pythagoreans, was, to a degree, called forth as a natural reaction against the new religion—to what many Pagans of Pythagorean persuasion perceived as Christianity's limited perspectives, narrow intolerance, and much flawed sense of ethic. As Andrew Smith observes,[32] Porphyry perceives, behind the surface of things, a "Via Universalis" shared by all peoples, a path common to the inhabitants of both the Greco-Roman world and to India, but lacking in the narrow exclusiveness and literalism of Christianity.

In the twilight of the Classical Greco-Roman world, all that was most noble in the culture and civilization that it represented became a focal point in the struggle of persons like Porphyry to stem the tide of Christianity. Nor were their efforts lost among the more cultured elements of Roman society. Heeding Porphyry's exhortation to adopt the Pythagorean diet, the Roman emperor, Rogetianus, for instance, was cured of gout.

Although today Porphyry is known chiefly for his *Life of Plotinus*, his greatest work is said to have been his calmly-reasoned 15 volume refutation of Christianity, *Against the Christians*. This in-depth study is no longer extant inasmuch as both the original and all copies were diligently sought out and destroyed by the Christians in centuries following.

As for Porphyry's *De Abstentia* or *On Abstinence From Animal Flesh*, it has, rather suprisingly, survived. For most modern readers, however, this volume is somewhat confusing inasmuch as as it presents both the pros and cons of the subject, all related within a bewildering maze of facts and objective historical descriptions. Yet, hidden here and there in the voluminous text are some gems of wisdom for the vegetarian. It is particularly in the last chapter that the vegetarian and anti-animal sacrifice perspective are clearly and emphatically presented.

Porphyry's own position is made quite clear in his discussion of the great Triptolemus whom he terms "the most ancient of Athenian legislators." Among the laws established by Triptolemus for the inhabitants of Athens, states Porphyry, was one which commands the following: "Sacrifice to the Gods from the fruits of the earth; injure not the animals."[33]

Thus, according to Porphyry, the observance of a vegetarian diet was, in fact, ordained by Triptolemus in his legal statute which forbade the injury of animals. Although this injunction was later violated, the philosopher, Xenocrates notes that such a law was still observed in his own time in Eleuses. Porphyry also observes that among the laws of Draco for the inhabitants of Attica was one which explicitly commanded that sacrifices to the Gods and heroes consist *only of* first fruits and cakes of flour. He mentions, too, that Dichaearchus notes that the most ancient men— the "golden men" of the "Golden Age" who were "generated through an alliance with the Gods"—were neither sacrificers of animals nor eaters of animals.[34] Indeed, he reminds us that in Dichaearchus and in ancient Greek thought in general there exists the idea that a vegetarian diet and a non-harming of animals go hand in hand with peace, justice, and harmony in human society.[35]

Porphyry cites numerous historical examples to support his contention that vegetarianism widely prevailed in Greece and elsewhere among the ancients. Euripedes, he notes, observes that many inhabitants of Crete "slay no animals for food."[36] Porphyry also mentions that the Zoroastrian priestly caste of ancient Persia abstained from both slaying and eating animals, including fish, as also did the brahmans of India and some of the priestly orders of ancient Egypt.

Like Plutarch, Porphyry viewed the slaying and consumption of animal flesh as a "defilement." Abstention from the eating of animals, and hence not being a party to their suffering and cruel deprivation of life, was seen as essential in the attainment of inner purification involving a state of peaceful harmony with all sentient beings. It may be noted that unlike many of the great Hellenic vegetarians of earlier periods, Porphyry did *not* subscribe to the notion of trans-specie soul-migration.

Porphyry emphatically condemns animal sacrifice as being essentially the same as the sacrifice of human life. Malific spirits, he notes, are drawn to blood sacrifice—to the monstrous act itself, to the heart-rending cries, to the odours, to the cadavers themselves, and—by extension, it may be observed—to the very idea or concept of blood sacrifice as an efficacious act.

That animal sacrifice was an established practice among nearly all primitivistic religious systems is, of course, well known. Nevertheless, that it continued for centuries within Greco-Roman Paganism as a major rite in the majority of temples for centuries after the great Pythagoras and numerous other philosophers and spiritual leaders had so pointedly condemned it, can only astonish us. Indeed, animal sacrifice should have been seen as the degenerate unethical monstrousity that it was and consequently excised like a cancerous growth from the rites of the old Paganism at all levels, thus returning to the high level of the primordial past——that distant time still present in the human consciousness as an archetypal memory—the "Golden Age" wherein *the only mode of sacrifice was with fruits and grains and cakes and fragrant resins.*

As Porphyry pointed out, Pythagoras, who sought to re-establish the "Golden Age" in his own time, decreed that *"No animal is to be sacrificed*; but that fruits are to be offered with meal and honey and the vegetable productions of the earth."[37]

Theophrastes, too, is cited by Porphyry as arguing against the sacrifice of animals, declaring that "blood sacrifice" is *not* "a worthy sacrifice to the Gods."[38] To conclude this section on Porphyry's contribution to the Great Pagan Vegetarian Revival, the following words seem singularly appropriate:

> For neither is it proper that the altars of the Gods should be defiled with murder nor that food of this kind should be allowed by men, as neither is it fit that men should eat one another.[39]

Other prominent figures who observed the vegetarian way of life during the last period of the old Greco-Roman civilization included the Neo-Platonist, Phoclydes; the notably anti-Christian Hierocles of Alexandria who was a student of Plutarch and was the author of not only a commentary on the *Chrysa Epe* or *Golden Words* of Pythagoras, but also of a condemnation of Christianity entitled, *Lover of Truth*; and Celus, who emphasized man's kinship with the animals, and the earth as the heritage of the animals no less than of man. Celus, too, wrote a refutation of Christianity, this tome being entitled *True Reason.*

7. *Buddhist Vegetarianism in the Far East*

1ST–13TH CENTURY A.D.

(A)   THE DEVELOPMENT OF A CHINESE BUDDHIST VEGETARIAN TRADITION—THE HISTORICAL BACKGROUND

While the Pagan Vegetarian Revival was occurring in the Greco-Roman world of the West, vegetarianism as an adjunct and observance of Buddhism was spreading throughout China. Buddhism was introduced into China during the 1st century A.D., and with it, there came into being in China, for the first time, a vegetarian ethic and perspective which hithertofore had not existed within the context of Chinese life and culture. Although non-Buddhist Chinese were and are notably non-vegetarian, Chinese Buddhists were to become the strictest vegetarians of the Buddhist world. Actually, Buddhist vegetarianism "flew in the face" of Confucian and Taoist tradition. Confucianism, for instance—which concerned itself with the "proper ordering" of life and society—did not include the animal world within its highly-structured ethical system, even maintaining a viewpoint not unlike that of Christianity, namely that man had no ethical obligation whatever to the animal world and that Heaven had given man the animals for his benefit and to do with as he liked.

Taoism was a far more complicated matter. On one hand, philosophical Taoism viewed the human and animal worlds as one within a balanced and harmonious Nature. Furthermore, it was sensitive to an ethic encompassing the whole of Nature. On the other hand, on a very exoteric level, as a popular religious cult embodying the most ancient traditions of Chinese folk religion, Taoism was not lacking in many primitivistic practices, including even animal sacrifice. Naturally, Buddhism strongly opposed the latter and eventually succeeded in bringing about the substitution of paper monkeys for real ones in popular Taoist rites.

It was only gradually that Buddhism made some small head-way among the people of China. This great religious tradition came to China in two ways—firstly via the fabled Silk or Spice Route from Central Asia where it had been introduced much ear-lier than in China, and secondly, directly from India. In both cases, the observance of a strictly vegetarian diet—a characteristic of Buddhism in its original Indian form, as we have seen, remained very much an important aspect of the ethics and way of life which Buddhism required of its adherents. Thus, from its inception, Bud-dhism in China was intimately involved with vegetarian ethic and practice.

By the year 68 A.D., both Buddhist sacred texts from India and Indian scholars capable of interpreting them in Chinese were present at the Chinese capital at Loyang. During the next three cen-turies, there was also an increasing influx of Buddhism into China via the Central Asian trade routes. Not a few of the merchants and their retainers who travelled the immense distances between East and West with camel caravans laden with exotic luxury items as well as daily necessities were Central Asians who had adopted the Buddhist Faith. Indeed, we tend to forget that Buddhism at one time had penetrated well into Afganistan and even into Persia, not to mention Turkestan. The very fact that some of these merchants were Buddhists indicates that even then, Buddhism had gone far beyond the strictly monastic confines so characteristic of it in its early days in India and later in Southeast Asia. In other words, the Buddhist mission was already, by that time, seen as involving the whole of society and human culture.

Numerous Buddhist temples and monasteries were con-structed along the Silk Route, east of Turfan. Outside of Bezeklek, finely wrought wooden superstructures built over exterior cliffs concealed elaborate cave temples, rooms, and corridors at Tianlang Shan. So too, at Dunhuang, along China's western frontier in Gansu Provence, a marvellous complex of cave temples with superb fres-coes came into existence. All of these served in the extension of the Buddhist mission to secular society, functioning as welcoming hos-pices and oases of spiritual sustenence where travellers of all sorts, including the numerous merchants, could rest during their arduous journeys and replenish their beings with Buddhist teachings of Compassion and healthful vegetarian fare.

With the collapse of the Han Dynasty, a number of Turkic and Tartar invasions occurred in Far Western China, and in 386 A.D., the Northern Wei Dynasty was established under the aegis of a Turkic people known as the Toba. The Toba Emperor, Tai Zi (r. 386-409 A.D.) together with most of his people, embraced Buddhism. During the period of peace which ensued, Buddhism prospered and the ethical vegetarianism which it advanced become the normal way of life throughout the lands under Northern Wei rule and considerably beyond it. The extraordinary "Mid-Air" or "Hanging Temples" of Mount Hengshan were built, and in 401, the monk Kumarajiva brought a major Mahayana scripture, the *Prajnaparamita Sutra* to China from Central Asia.

Nearly a century after the Emperor Tai Zi's conversion to Buddhism in the north, in south-central China, the Emperor Wu Ti, who reigned between 502 and 549 A.D., became an outstanding patron and propagator of Buddhism and the vegetarian way of life. During his long reign, this great emperor did all in his power to advance Buddhism and its ethics of compassion in China. Not without reason, is he sometimes termed "the Imperial Bodhisattva." Proclaiming a "New Era of Mercy and Compassion," Emperor Wu Ti banned every type of meat from the imperial table and urged his subjects to follow his example and adopt a strictly vegetarian diet, noting that those who eat the meat of animals killed by others bring the same karmic retribution upon themselves as the actual killers. He then forbade the use of animals for medicinal purposes as well as for ritual sacrifice in popular Taoism. Actively manifesting Buddhist compassion in all aspects of life, Wu Ti proceeded to release prisoners and ordered the building of innumerable temples, hospitals, and clinics throughout his realm.

Although during the Sui Dynasty, which was founded in 581, Buddhism acquired an increasingly wide following among both the aristocracy and the scholarly elite, it was during the T'ang Dynasty (618-906 A.D.), that Buddhism—and hence the widespread observance of a vegetarian diet—reached its zenith in China.

During the T'ang Dynasty, Turkestan, Mongolia, Manchuria, and Korea were all absorbed into the Middle Kingdom (China). Ethnic strife and factionalism was laid aside in an all-embracing unity. It was also a period of social change in which a vast civil service apparatus came into existence and became a major force in government administration. Inasmuch as the the individuals involved in this civil service were persons of exceptional literary and aesthetic background, a very high cultural level was ensured throughout the period.

The intellectual and artistic productions of the T'ang represented a fusion of influences and styles, those of China's own past merging with those from abroad—from India, Persia, and Central Asia. The T'ang was a period of exceptional creativity which was characterized by a profound aesthetic sensitivity and refinement. It was also a period of great innovation when the process of woodblock printing was invented by Chinese Buddhists, the earliest surviving printed book on the planet Earth being the *Diamond Sutra* which was produced in T'ang Dynasty China in the year 868 A.D. It was produced for "universal free distribution." One may note, too, that the T'ang represented a high point in trade and commercial involvement with the outside world as well as between the very diverse peoples within the T'ang Empire itself.

Intellectually and spiritually, the creativeness of the T'ang was manifest in the specific forms and perspectives taken by Chinese Buddhism during the period. Many new "schools" of Buddhist thought and practice came into being. These ranged from Pure Land or "Jingtu" with its cult of Amito-Fo and Kwanyin (perhaps indicative of a growing concern for animals of whom Kwanyin is seen as the Patron and Protector) to the Chan or Zen school, which, although its origins are said to date to the 6th century, only took on its mature form during the T'ang. All were, by the way, strictly vegetarian in observance.

When we consider the fact that Chang'an (the T'ang capital) was the largest city in the world at that time with a population of close to 2 million inhabitants, at least half of whom are estimated to have been observant Buddhists, one can picture a predominently vegetarian population of 1 million or more, existing within the context of a supremely civilized milleu wherein a highly stylized etiquette, an elegant aesthetic, a depth of learning, and a keen sensitivity to Nature and the arts all merged to produce one of the highest points of human civilization. It was such phenomena as these which so captivated the Japanese who adopted and cultivated many aspects of T'ang culture, aesthetic, and custom—preserving them almost as though in a museum, as it were, even until the present century.

One may note that the the majority of theatrical and musical forms and themes present even today in Chinese, Japanese, and Korean culture derive from those created and developed during the T'ang. T'ang creativity, with its considerable Buddhist vegetarian input, is also to be observed in the painting, sculpture, architecture, porcelain, and gardens of the T'ang era. Many of these T'ang productions are considered to be among the finest in human history. Poetry of the period, too, was not lacking in Buddhist vegetarian input. In fact, the greatest T'ang poet, Wang Wei (699-759 A.D. or alternative dates, 701-765 A.D.)—who was also a notable painter, scholar, and one-time official at the T'ang Court—was a devout Buddhist who emphasized as a major theme, man's ideal harmony with Nature. Liu Yu-hsi (772-843) was another prominent Buddhist poet of the period. Thus, despite Buddhism's original monastic orientation, as early as the T'ang Dynasty, it very clearly gave evidence of its ability to inspire and contribute to human culture and society in a wide variety of creative endeavours. To the extent that the persons involved were observant Buddhists, they were, of course, vegetarians. Indeed, it might be said that many of the great cultural and artistic achievements of the T'ang owed their origins to persons who followed the vegetarian way of life.

The longer Buddhism was in China, the more thoroughly Sinified it became. Thus, in the Middle Kingdom, it became less ascetic in orientation and more integrated into family life and society itself. While monks and monasteries retained their importance, Buddhism penetrated the whole fabric of Chinese cultural life, leaving its impress on lay society. While maintaining a strictly vegetarian diet, Chinese Buddhists by no means disavowed the characteristic Chinese love of food and culinary art. Instead, they seized upon every possible excuse to hold elaborate "vegetarian banquets."

During much of the T'ang Dynasty, a large percentage of the population—ranging from aristocrats and merchants to artists, craftsmen, and peasant farmers—are said to have been observant Buddhists, and hence vegetarians. Yet, while Buddhism was clearly a major religious influence in Chinese life for much of the T'ang, its fortunes were by no means consistent throughout the period. For one thing, there were fluctuations in regard to imperial patronage itself. The Li family, who were founders of the dynasty, after all, traced their decent to Lao-Tzu. What is more, Confucianism remained very much part of the government apparatus throughout the dynasty. While some emperors and members of the imperial

family did become devout Buddhists, or in some cases sympa-
thizers, others remained emphatically non-Buddhist, despite the
widespread growth of Buddhism among their people. At times,
there were even persecutions and suppressions, such as those
which occurred between 843 and 845. How different had been the
reign of the pious, but greatly maligned and slandered Empress, Wu
Chiao (Wu Hou, posthumous) who occupied the Imperial Throne
from 680 to 705 A.D., notwithstanding vehement opposition to her
both as a Buddhist and as a female ruler on the part of the Confu-
cianist scholars and government officials.

As for the Emperor Tai-Tsung (r. 763-779), not only was he
devoutly Buddhist, but most of his government officials were as
well. It was during his reign that Chang'an became a notable centre
of Buddhism, indeed a model Buddhist city with Buddhists engaging in numerous meritorious endeavours under the guidance of the
monk, Amoghavajra. These included the erection of shrines and
temples, the copying of sutras, and the arrangement of vast vegetarian feasts in memory of the dead and given as well to assist the
poor. At these feasts, meals were served to 10,000 people or more.
Hospital complexes to help the poor and the aged free of charge
were also constructed.

Despite the fact that by the end of the T'ang, Buddhism—and
hence the vegetarian way of life—had left an indelible imprint upon Chinese life and civilization, a gradual decline of both
set in. Indeed, aside from a brief period between 1308 and 1312
when the Emperor Wu-tsung attempted to revive Buddhism, the
number of Buddhists and vegetarians became fewer and fewer
until the great Buddhist renaissance under the leadership of the
revered Chu-hung in the 16th century.

Fortunately, Buddhism in China, despite various persecutions,
was never to suffer the fate of that in India, the land of its origins
where its death knell was sounded by the brahmin, Kumarila
Bhatta, in the first half of the 8th century. Not only did Bhatta ini-
tiate a ruthless persecution of Buddhists in which many were slain,
but he also forced large numbers of Buddhists to embrace Hinduism against their wills, thus bringing Buddhism to an end on the
Indian continent.

As for the Tibetans, who accepted Buddhism only in the 8th
century, they came to differ very greatly from Chinese Mahayanists
inasmuch as they—while vaguely viewing vegetarianism as an

ideal—felt no obligation to observe such a diet, although a few, in fact, did so.

(B) ANOMALIES OF VEGETARIAN PRACTICE AMONG JAPANESE BUDDHISTS

Buddhism was introduced to Japan from the Middle Kingdom during the reign of the Japanese Emperor, Yomei, who ascended the Imperial Throne in 585 A.D. Eventually, Japan, rather than China where Buddhists became a minority after the end of the T'ang Dynasty, became the leading Mahayanist country.

Needless to say, we are not concerned here with the specific teachings of the many different schools of Buddhism which developed among the Japanese. Suffice it to say that the highly metaphysical Kegon School received extensive imperial patronage during the Nara Period. During the 8th and 9th centuries, other branches of the Mahayana came into ascendency in Japan. The Tendai School with its emphasis on the *Lotus Sutra* was brought to Kyoto from China by Saicho in the 8th century; Shingon, with its cult of Vairocana, the Buddha of the Sun, and its elaborate rituals was established by Kobo Daishi (774-835 A.D.). Both of these proved to be extremely popular with the Japanese people for many centuries to come. Some 400 years later, these older forms of the Mahayana were joined by the Zen or Ch'an School as well as the Amidist or Pure Land Schools of Shinran and Honen. Known as the Jodo-Shin and Shinshu Schools, these became the most popular forms of Buddhism in Japan and remain so today. Unfortunately, Pure Land Buddhism in Japan, unlike that of China, is notably non-vegetarian.

Chinese Buddhism, of course, brought with it to Japan, a strictly vegetarian dietary ethic—but, in Japan, certain ambiguities very soon developed in this respect, setting Japanese Buddhism apart from the strict vegetarian observance which prevailed in Chinese Buddhism. The problem in this regard stemmed first and foremost from the inordinate Japanese fondness for fish as a food. This predelection, in fact, seemed (and indeed, still seems) to amount to something of a national "passion." What is more, the fishing and boat building industries both were and are of major importance to the whole Japanese economy. Consequently, Chinese Buddhist exhortations to abstain from fish, to a large degree, fell on deaf ears.

The fact is that, aside from their consumption of fish, the Japanese of that period—and indeed right up to the present century—were essentially "vegetarian" to begin with. Neither mammals nor birds were considered by the overwhelming majority of pre-modern Japanese to be either acceptable or desirable as a "food." That the consumption of such animals was seen as a repulsive and aesthetically-repellent act by most Japanese must have both surprised and delighted the Chinese Buddhist missionaries who were used to having to combat the Chinese penchant for eating the flesh of pigs and ducks. Thus, while urging the Japanese to desist from eating fish, they apparently did not make a major point of the matter, no doubt assuming that eventually the Japanese passion for eating fish would simply drop off. Of course, it did not.

In consequence, while a strictly vegetarian diet, including a proscription of fish, was held up *as a desirable ideal,* in the end, this ideal was, in fact, practiced only by a few monks and occasional lay persons of exceptional piety. Here, it may be noted that Zen Buddhism, with its particular emphasis on the *Lankavatara Sutra*—a major source of Buddhist vegetarian precepts—has always encouraged a strictly vegetarian diet, particularly in its monasteries.

Although the average Japanese Buddhist of whatever school in, say, the year 1200, would have strictly avoided the eating of birds and mammals—both through natural aversion and Buddhist ethical prohibition, few indeed refrained from eating fish. Thus, while some Japanese Buddhists have over the centuries been strictly vegetarian, others have abstained from warm-blooded animals, but not from fish. Unfortunately, still others—indeed, the majority today, notably those who are followers of the Pure Land or Shinshu School, claim that they are "too weak" or "too sinful" to observe a vegetarian diet at all. Consequently, such persons consume not only fish but all manner of warm-blooded animals which have become common in Japanese cuisine since the influx of Western ways and customs to that country during the present century, particularly during and after the American Occupation.

8. The Eclipse of Vegetarianism in the West— The Historical Background and Official Christian Attitudes

c. 3rd–15TH CENTURY A.D.

As we have noted in Chapter 6, a Pagan Vegetarian Revival of considerable strength began during the last decades prior to the appearance of Christianity. This vegetarian revival gained momentum as the old Paganism struggled to assert itself against the increasingly powerful Christian Church. Thus, during the period which lasted for the first 400 years of Christianity, the advocacy and observance of a strictly vegetarian diet often went hand in hand with a deeply-rooted opposition to Christianity and the concepts and world view which it stood for. Indeed, this was a time when a veritable re-naissance of the ancient philosophically-based ethically-oriented Pythagorean vegetarianism occurred among wide segments of the population.

Although the old Paganism in its various forms tended to be both tolerant and syncretistic in its approach, the Christianity of the day was exactly the opposite. Indeed, it was stridently aggressive in its proselytism as well as in its condemnation of other spiritual paths and perspectives. This intolerance, in turn, provoked and drew back upon it a certain intolerance on the part of the Pagans who—faced with the insistence by the Christians that they alone represented "the Truth"—forgot their own traditional syncretist tolerance. Thus, policies were initiated which aimed at curtailing the Christian Church, culminating in the persecutions under Diocletion.

With the coming to the throne of Constantine (r. 306-337 A.D.), however, the situation was reversed and the Christians began their assault on the Old Religion. Indeed, the official absolutist State Church, with an all-powerful emperor and hierarchy directing its course, proceeded to set the tone and measure, as it were, eventually gaining complete control over European life and culture, customs and ethics—first among the Mediterranean peoples and later extending its dominion into the North as well. As entire populations adopted its beliefs and codes of behaviour, many survivals of the ancient Greco-Roman civilization—including an ethically-oriented, philosophically-based vegetarianism—entered into sharp decline and eventual oblivion.

At this point it is necessary to examine Christianity's official attitude towards the observance of a vegetarian diet and to assess its general opposition to the old Pythagorean vegetarianism. The curious fact is that the orthodox Christianity of the official State Church, although opposed to animal sacrifice as a religious rite, was quite lacking in any sense whatever of the serious ethical transgression involved in the harming, hurting, and killing of animal victims! According to Christian theology, God made the animals "subject unto man," who was free to use and exploit them as he liked with total ethical impunity! Augustine of Hyppo, for instance, believed that animals lack the "reasoning faculty" and that consequently, mankind need not concern itself with animal suffering (see p. 187, *The City of God, Against the Pagans*, V. 6. William Chase Greene, trans. Cambridge, Mass., 1969).

In all fairness, however, it may be observed that *occasional* Christian individuals contradicted the general Christian disregard for non-human life forms. The 4th century Byzantine Greek hierarch and codifier of Eastern Christian monasticism, Basil of Caesaria, for instance, urged treating all animals with kindness and even developing a sense of fellowship with them.[40] So too, various desert and forest hermits over the centuries were notably compassionate in their dealings with wild animals. Such examples, however, are quite exceptional—individual manifestations which, while indicating an enlightened kindliness on the part of the persons concerned, by no means revealed any sense of ethical obligation towards the animal world on the part of the official Church. To the contrary, one might say any compassionate actions towards animals manifest by individual Christians occurred not due to any qualities or precepts inherent in Christian ethic, but rather *inspite of the official Christian position and perspective.*

Inasmuch as Clement of Alexandria (150-215 A.D.) is sometimes cited as a supporter of vegetarianism, it is necessary to point out here that this is hardly the case. Although, it might be said that

Clement maintained a somewhat more "liberal" view towards a veg-etarian diet than was common among most Christians of his day, he by no means advocated such a diet as incumbant upon all. Like nearly all Christians, he was blind to the ethical values involved here. His discourse on food in his work *The Instructor*[41] does, how-ever, provide us with an illustration of the orthodox Christian atti-tude towards vegetarianism and diet in general as it was to prevail over the centuries.

It may be observed to begin with that Clement of Alexandria's perspective in regard to food is essentially ascetic. He makes it quite clear that he is, in fact, opposed to what he terms "luxury foods," "dainties from beyond the seas," condiments, sugar plums, honey cakes, and even "pastry making"—equating all of these with "mis-chevious pleasures." Cooking itself, he decries as "an unhappy art." While he does state that "it is good not to eat flesh" (from which term, he excludes fish, by the way), he quite clearly states that if one does (eat flesh), "he does not sin." Noting that according to tradition, Matthew "partook of seeds, nuts, and vegetables without flesh," he also quotes Matthew XV-II as being representative of the Christian perspective on the matter—"For it is not that which entereth in that defileth a man, but that which goeth out of his mouth" (which is to say, lies and slanders). In other words, accord-ing to Clement and the Christian scriptures, the *kind* of food eaten is a matter of ethical indifference; there is no sense of the ethical violation involved in the killing and eating of animals. Even more than "meat," Clement objects to "luxury foods." He is an advocate of a frugal diet which excludes even "desserts" and "honey cakes." Although Clement states that it is "best," but not necessary, to avoid "animal flesh," by which he signifies the flesh of birds and mam-mals, he clearly manifests Christianity's essential insensitivity to fish as living beings as well as its stubborn illogic in refusing to acknowledge that fish is "flesh." *He, in fact, cites fish and bread together as "beautiful examples of simple food!"* The Christian, after all, could hardly reject fish as food. Jesus consorted with fishermen and forbade them not. So too, his chief apostle, Peter, was a fisher-man. What is more, according to Christian legend, Jesus fed the multitudes on "loaves and fishes," and is said to have eaten "broiled fish" himself after his "resurrection."

In view of the above, there can be no gainsaying of the fact that the orthodox Christian perspective in regard to diet and the

taking of animal life, even at its best, is at the opposite end of the
spectrum from that of the great "father of vegetarianism" in the
West, Pythagoras, who, according to tradition, took such joy in pur-
chasing whole nets-full of fish from the fishermen in order to release them in their life-giving element, the sea—a beautiful custom
which, one may note, was also, much later, to become a major
aspect of Chinese Buddhist practice, particularly under the revered
Chu-hung.

The extent to which traditional Christianity is at odds with a
genuine vegetarian perspective is also made quite clear in the scrip-
tural passage (Acts X, 10-15), quoted by Clement, concerning the
"trance" of Peter—"And he saw heaven opened and a vessel let
down on the earth . . . and all the four-footed beasts and creeping
things of the earth and the fowls of heaven in it; and there came a
voice saying 'Rise, slay, and eat.'" Peter declines, saying that he eats
not that which is "common or unclean," perhaps referring to pigs
among the four-footed beasts. Thereupon, a voice rebuked him
with the words: "What God hath cleansed, call not common." Thus,
states Clement, "the use of them (that is, any or all animal species)
is accordingly indifferent to us."[42] Not once does Clement address
the ethical issue involved in the taking of animal life and, by extension, the eating of "meat," or more bluntly and honestly put, the
eating of animals.

The fact is that when Christianity—in its early centuries, during the Middle Ages, Medieval Period, and later—required abstinence from animal flesh, as on certain days of fasting or among a
certain element of its membership, as for instance, monks, it did so
for entirely "ascetic" reasons. There was no concern whatever for
the animals involved or any sense of doing wrong in killing animal
beings! Nor did fasting from animal flesh occur out of any sense of
health or nutrition. Rather astonishingly, seasonal and monastic
fasting from meat within the orthodox Christianity of both East and
West was conceived of solely in terms of "self-denial," as an ascetic
abstention from something not only permissable (as on feast days),
but desirable in itself!

As close as the official Christian Church came to endorsing a
vegetarian diet was in the requirement of Greek or Eastern monasticism that monks and nuns permanently abstain from warm-
blooded animals, both birds and mammals, for ascetic reasons.
As we have observed, however, *this proscription by no means*

included fish, which except for the highest level of monastics—namely, the "schema monks" or "hermits of the great vow" (actually so few in number as to be all but non-existent)—was not only permitted but consummed in great quantities on feast days, thus flying in the face of Pythagorean tradition. Similar rules of diet are said to have prevailed among the *early* Benedictines in the West.

As for lay people, they were expected to abstain from animal flesh—sometimes including fish and sometimes excluding it—*only on specified "fast days"* and during designated penitential seasons. Outside of these "official" contexts, a strictly vegetarian diet would have been looked upon with considerable suspicion and decided disapproval. One might surmise that if any lay person decided to follow an uncompromisingly vegetarian diet on a permanent basis for reasons of conscience or ethic, just about the only way he or she could have done so would have been either as a "penance" for some particularly "heinous sin," or on the excuse that his or her health required it. Otherwise, such vegetarian observance would have been viewed as possibly, or even probably, indicative of "heterodox" views of one sort or another.

Vegetarianism in its deepest roots involved and was intimately connected with the rejection of "blood sacrifice," including its efficacy as a symbol. Thus, it is quite likely that opposition to an ethically-based vegetarianism on the part of traditional or "official" Christianity derives, at least on one level, from the essential vegetarian rejection of the primitive idea of "blood sacrifice," consequently calling into question that basic dogma of traditional Christianity—the "blood sacrifice of the cross" and its supposed efficacy as a "redemptive act," as well as the eucharistic rites which form the basis of its cultus. The official or "orthodox" Christianity of the day actually had far more in common with the predominant current of the Greco-Roman Paganism than is commonly admitted. Orthodox Christianity itself perpetuated the concept of "blood sacrifice" as an efficacious act. Indeed, its whole theological perspective was structured to fit the primitivistic notion of "blood sacrifice!" What is more, while Christianity objected to actual animal sacrifice on a cultic level, it nevertheless had no objection whatever to its adherents killing animals "for table," so long as they were eaten on "feast days" and not on specified "fast days."

When the nephew of Constantine, Julian "the Apostate" (331-363 A.D.) inherited the throne of Constantinople in the year 361, he

sought to revive the ancient Greco-Roman Paganism, re-establish-
ing it by edict in 362. After initially inclining towards the "Pythagorean diet" and ethic, Julian very soon abandoned them, choosing
to ignore the great Greco-Roman vegetarian tradition and sense of
ethical obligation towards the animal world, instead promoting a
widespread revival of animal sacrifice (a practice which had been
dying out among observant Pagans for several centuries) as a necessary adjunct of the cult! Thus, Julian distanced himself from the
noblest traditions within the Old Paganism, choosing instead to
propagate the worst.

Julian died in 362, and although the Emperor Jovian was tolerant of all religions, the "pious" Theodosius (r. 379-395), backed by
the hierarchy of the Church, in the year 381 began a full-scale persecution of the ancient Paganism. Throughout the Empire, Christian
zealots, often with monks as major participants or even instigators,
attacked and looted the old temples and holy places, even murdering many Pagan devotees.

In their narrow fanaticism, orthodox Christians not only
sought to destroy all manifestations of the ancient Paganism, but the
culture and and customs which had grown out of it as well, ethical
vegetarianism included. Even such phenomena as the olympic
games or competitions were condemned on the grounds that they
were "Pagan in origin," "too carnal" in nature, and "corrupted the
morals" of both onlookers and participants! While the barbaric
gladitorial combats between men were stopped—as indeed urged
long before by the great Pagan Humanist and vegetarian,
Plutarch—the savage spectacle of fights between animals were
allowed by the Christians to continue for centuries with virtually no
one calling for their cessation.

Rather suprisingly, the Athens Academy, a major centre of
Pagan learning and philosophy, remained in operation until
Justinian's widespread persecutions in 529, at which time its
millenial history ended. With its passing, the enlightened philosophically-based Pythagorean vegetarianism of the ancient Greco-
Roman world, as practiced by many of the Academy's members,
entered into oblivion.

In short, the basis of the eclipse of the Greco-Roman vegetarian tradition lay in the triumph of Christianity as the official "State
Religion" and its putting down, on the part of both the emperors
and the ecclesiastical hierarchy, of the Old Religion and culture in

all its forms and currents, both positive and negative. Consequently, for over a thousand years, vegetarianism virtually disappeared from Europe! It may be suggested, however, that at least a few clandestine followers of Pythagoras remained in existence during this entire period, maintaining a vegetarian diet and other positive aspects of the Old Paganism *behind the scenes*, as it were. No doubt, such did exist, at least as an "underground" current in the Byzantine East.

On the farthest fringes of the official or "orthodox" Christian Church of both East and West, from its earliest days right up through the Medieval Period, there were many small and often very localized sects and movements, some of which observed a vegetarian diet within the broader spectrum of their general opposition to the official Church. These movements were mostly Gnostic or Manichean in orientation and included such groups as the Bogomils in the East and the Cathars in the West. Some of these groups— quite aside from from their adherence to a vegetarian diet—held certain extremist views (as in their condemnation of the material world as "evil" and their opposition to both procreation and the legitimacy of private property) that only served to increase the general antagonism of the official Church to the vegetarian mode of diet in any but a monastic-ascetic context or on prescribed days of fasting.

The Trappists, a notably strict order of monks, founded in 1093, afford a rather curious example of vegetarian observance within the context of Roman Catholic Christianity. Their abstention from animal flesh is entirely ascetic in nature, being viewed by them as a "privation" to the end of "curbing the passions." Neither ethics, philosophy, or health and nutrition enter into the matter. The extent to which the vegetarianism observed by the Trappists differs from that which prevailed in the ancient Greco-Roman world or in India and the Far East is very forcefully brought to our attention by the fact that despite their vegetarian diet, the Trappists nevertheless thought nothing of raising and selling male "veal calves" for table as a means of supporting their monasteries, these calves being an incidental "by-product" of their well-known cheese industry! There is something rather outstandingly grotesque in such a situation.

One might have expected a vegetarian tradition to have developed among the Franciscans in the 13th century. Such, however, was not the case. Although later noted as a "patron saint"' of animals, *Francis of Assisi was not himself a vegetarian!* Nor was the observance of a vegetarian diet among the rules of the Franciscan Order. As for the theology of the Dominican, Thomas Aquinas, who was strongly influenced by Aristotle's derogatory views of animal being, he helped to fuel the official Church's denial of man's moral obligation to the animal world as well as its bias against an ethically-based vegetarianism. The inescapable fact is that throughout its history, "official" mainstream Christianity has regarded animals as no more than a means to an end—namely, the end of being exploited by man for whatever purpose he wishes.

9. The Return to the Greco-Roman Past in the Italian Renaissance

15th-16th Centuries

We have already mentioned the ancient idea of the "Golden Age" and its relationship to the practice of vegetarianism in the first chapter of this study. After its eclipse for some 900 years, dating from the reign of Justinian, the idea of the "Golden Age"—as conceived by the ancient Greeks—again came to the surface of the human consciousness in the Italian Renaissance. This was particularly true in Firenze during the reign and at the Court of Lorenzo de Medici (r. 1468-1492), whose motto was "Le Tems revient" (Old French) or "The Times have returned." "The Times" indicated the Pagan Greco-Roman past, and by extension, the primordial archetypal past known as the "Golden Age." During the Italian Renaissance, as indeed in the ancient Greco-Roman world itself, a variety of ideals and characteristics were superimposed on the "Golden Age" in accord with individual predelections.*

For some, the fabled "Lost Continent of Atlantis," with its high civilization, was, at its peak, the embodiment of the "Golden Age;" for others, that age was perceived in terms of an idyllic "rustic life" of great simplicity. Herein lay the roots of the "Back to Nature" ideal which came to play such an important part in the vegetarian revival of the 19th century as it emerged in connection with an awareness of the "Golden Age" in mankind's remote past. In other words, it was out of the Renaissance consciousness and its great Humanist perspectives and insights that the rebirth of vegetarianism in the West eventually evolved during the 18th and 19th centuries.

* It may be observed that in still later centuries, the whole original notion of the "Golden Age" was totally perverted by the projection of hunting and fishing activities on its inhabitants. Other distortions were even evident in the ancient world itself. Pindar, for example, taught that the "Golden Age" only became a reality after death, in a "life beyond."

The attempted "return" to the "Golden Age," which occurred during the Renaissance, was multi-faceted in its expression. For instance, the beauty of the nude human body again assumed its proper place in aesthetics, and marvellous sculptures and paintings, embodying the Greco-Roman past and its Gods and heros, were created. The ancient Classical culture was making a "comeback," and side by side with paintings which involved Christian subject matter, painters such as Sandro Botichelli produced superb images of the old Gods. In this regard, his "Primavera," intended as a symbolic embodiment of the times, comes readily to mind. Here, the handsome God, Mercurios or Mercury—depicted here as Lorenzo's brother, Guillamo—is shown with the Three Muses as well as a resplendent "Spring."

While attempts were made to revive the ancient music with sung recitals of Classical poems and epics performed to the accompaniment of the "orphic lyre," superbly symmetrical gardens—sometimes involving highly contrived "natural scenes" and grottoes—were laid out. A veritable "cult" of flowers and plants, particularly those of exotic origins, came into being together with a newly-developed "theriophilly" or "fondness for animals." The latter is manifest in the *Menageri* of Lorenzo De Medici, whose poetry reveals a boundless delight in the multiplicity and ways of animals. A new sensitivity and respect for the animal world was coming into being. Lastly, one may mention as an integral part of Renaissance Humanism, the magnificent sense of theatre, symbolism, and aesthetics which were cultivated within the context of a Neoplatonist metaphysic. In all of the above phenomena, the feeling was that the ancient "Golden Age" had returned.

Thanks to a greater openess in regard to human sexuality in general, including its homosexual aspect, a more tolerant and healthy society came into being, at least within the setting of the high civilization and stylized elegance of Lorenzo's Court and the Platonic Academy, which sought to re-create the atmosphere and spirit of ancient Greece. In this, as in the previously-described characteristics of the age, Renaissance Italy—particularly Firenze or Florence—seemed very near indeed to returning to the more natural perspectives of the ancient Pagan culture. Although the Christian cult was still observed on the surface, it seemed little more than a "frosting," as it were.

Unfortunately, the whole process referred to above was brought to a grinding halt by the mad monk, Savonarola and his fanatical rabble of followers who, after the death of the great Lorenzo, seized power in the city of Firenze and established a puritanical fascist Christian "theocracy" not unlike that of Oliver Cromwell in England about 150 years later.

Having made himself the "watchdog" of public morality, Savonarola sought to force his narrowly puritanical and sexually-inhibited views on the whole of society. To this end, he suppressed the revival of the ancient Greco-Roman culture, closed down the theatres, and ordered the destruction of musical instruments as well as of all paintings and statuary which depicted human nudity and the ancient Gods. He also instigated gangs of street thugs to make savage attacks on homosexuals!

If allowed to follow its natural course, the Greco-Roman renaissance of Lorenzo's time unquestionably would have led to a revival of vegetarianism. Indeed, the very, fact that the original "Golden Age" was viewed as non-carnivorous and as a time when animals were neither hunted nor sacrificed to the Gods, could only have led to a widespread turning to the "Pythagorean diet." Undoubtedly, at least a few persons within the rarified aesthetic-philosophical atmosphere of Lorenzo's Court and the Platonic Academy did, in fact, become vegetarians. Unfortunately, as far as the author is aware, there is no direct evidence concerning such a phenomenon.

Here, it may be suggested, too, that a secret or semi-secret Pythagorean Pagan Tradition had been preserved over the centuries, behind the scenes, as it were, within the life and civilization of Byzantium. In this respect, it is well to remind ourselves that the Italian Renaissance itself, with its revival of Greco-Roman culture was, after all, fueled and inspired to a considerable extent by the numerous Greek scholars who fled to Italy from Byzantium when Constantinople fell to the Turks in 1453, bringing with them a rebirth of the ancient Hellenic wisdom. Among the many aspects of this wisdom to which the West became exposed were the ethical principles of Pythagoras, including a strict proscription of the killing and eating of animals.

10. The Beginnings of a New Perspective in the West— Leonardo Da Vinci

1452-1519

Among those rare individuals who *did* adopt a vegetarian way of eating in the midst of the dominant Catholic Christian society with its suspicion of the ancient Pythagorean diet and its exclusion of the animal world from its ethic, was the great and rather enigmatic genius, Leonardo Da Vinci (1452-1519). Born in the Val d'Arno region of northern Italy, Leonardo was undoubtedly one of the most remarkable geniuses of human history. A leading figure of the Italian Renaissance, Leonardo Da Vinci contributed to most areas of human creativity. He was a masterful painter who had studied under Verrochio; an architect, engineer, and inventor; a musician who played the flute and sang like a professional; a philosopher who had familiarized himself with the wisdom and culture of the ancient Greco-Roman world; a scientist well versed not only in botany, but also in anatomy and geology.

That this remarkable individual who was in touch with the most profound intellectual currents of his time should have adopted a vegetarian diet should come as a surprise to no one. That his vegetarianism was well known among his countrymen is attested to by the fact that a certain Andrea Corsali, writing to Guiliano de Medici in 1515, speaks of the inhabitants of a certain part of India who, in the manner of Leonardo da Vinci, refrain from, the eating of animals.[43]

That Leonardo was fond of most animals and treated them with "kindness" and "consideration" is mentioned by Vasari. Notably concerned for the well-being of "quadrapeds," particularly sheep and oxen—which he excluded from his diet for a considerable portion of his life—he eventually also excluded birds. In the fashion of Pythagoras, he even came to derive a considerable degree of pleasure from saving the lives of birds destined for the table, buying them from the bird-sellers in the market place in order to set them free.

Although it has been suggested by some that Leonardo's eventual and gradual adoption of a thoroughly vegetarian diet was solely for "medical reasons," it is clear from his own words as well as from his buying and releasing of birds that it was a matter of ethics for him as well.

Living as he did during the Renaissance with its marvellous rebirth and flowering of the ancient Pagan wisdom and culture under Medici patronage, Leonardo unquestionably derived much within his vegetarian perspective from the ancients. The works of Plutarch, Plotinus, Porphyry, and Ovid—all advocates of vegetarianism—were among his small personal collection of books. We know, too, that he was not unfamiliar with the ancient Pythagorean wisdom in all its multi-faceted genius, ranging from astronomy to ethics. Zubov also mentions that Da Vinci was familiar with Ovid's presentation of Pythagoras in *The Metamorphoses*.[44]

With plain-spoken disgust, in his *Profetie*, Da Vinci refers to the keepers of estates eating their own workers, the latter designating the oxen which till the soil.[45] In eating animals, observes Da Vinci, man makes of himself a tomb, a house of the dead.

We have already noted his profound empathy with birds which he rejoiced to release from captivity as well as his sense of moral obligation towards sheep and oxen. Likewise, in his remarkable painting of the "Lady with an Ermine" ("Ritratto di Donna con Ermellino"), today in the Czartoryski Museum in Krakow, one can sense the painter's deep sensitivity towards this extraordinary little beast. The painting is as much a portrait of the ermine as it is a portrait of the lady. What is more, they each seem to reflect each other as though from some mirror within the depths of Da Vinci's own being. The painting is of particular interest to us here also inasmuch as the subject matter—an aristocratic lady with her tame pet ermine—indicates an expansion of human consciousness in regard to the animal world as well as an increase of sensitivity towards it, the ermine being portrayed as very much of an individual personality in himself and, one may add, a being very much deserving of our respect. Such are the sentiments which Da Vinci succeeds in conveying to the beholder.

Yet, the fact that Da Vinci's empathy with the animal world was not all-inclusive is quite clear from several incidents related in Vasari which indicate certain ambiguities in the great genius's personality. He quite clearly disliked such creatures as bats, newts, snakes, and flies—and was not benevolently disposed towards them. In this, Da Vinci remained very much a man of Medieval Europe and, despite a shared vegetarianism, very different from the ancient Pythagoreans as well as the Chinese Buddhists and Indian Jains whose reverence for life and respect for all sentient beings was of a very much broader and all-encompassing nature. In another respect, too, the great Da Vinci—who incidently wrote from right to left—manifested a certain ambivalence. Although noted for his "goodness" and even "sweetness" of character, according to Vasari, he was also the inventor of diverse lethal weapons! His last years were spent in France under the patronage of King Francis I.

Da Vinci was, in a sense, representative of the Renaissance consciousness in general. He was also very much of an "independent thinker," one whose mind and creativity reached out far beyond the narrow confines of Christian orthodoxy. As such, he was not afraid to contradict many of the generally-accepted Christian attitudes towards the animal world as well as the Church's abiding distrust of an ethically-based vegetarianism which it saw as both a survival of one current of the ancient Paganism and as the virtual hallmark of various sects and movements which it deemed "heterodox." Furthermore, the respect accorded to him as one of the leading creative geniuses of his day allowed Da Vinci to assume a somewhat non-conformist stance which would not have been tolerated in many others. The surprising thing is that more people within the Italian Renaissance milleu did not, like Da Vinci, return to the ancient "Pythagorean diet." Indeed, perhaps many did so, but rather than rousing the dragon of ecclesiastical disapproval, chose to maintain their vegetarian diet and the ethic and philosophy behind it on a very low-key level.

Here it may be observed that Leonardo and the other great Renaissance painters and sculptors of his time and before, despite the Christian subject matter of the majority of their paintings, were in fact in the process of "re-habilitating" and restoring—at least as archetypes and "maps" of human consciousness and experience— the ancient Gods and myths of the Greco-Roman past. What is more, the old Gods were often presented in forms interchangeable with individual figures of the Christian Pantheon. Da Vinci's "Bacco" (Bacchus or Dionysios), for instance, is alternately termed a "John the Forerunner." And, to cite a quite different artist of the period, one may ask if Michelangelo's "David" in Firenze is, in fact, anyone other than the great Apollo? The ancient Pagan appreciation of the beauty and wonder of Nature, of the human body itself, and of the animal world was reasserting itself despite years of suppression on the part of the Christian establishment. In all of this, a new Humanist perspective was being formed and the way being prepared for the advancement of the vegetarian way of life. Included in this perspective was an increasing sense of man's ethical obligation to treat both our fellow men and the diverse species of animals with kindness and compassion.

11. A Renaissance of Buddhist Vegetarianism in China—The Revered Chu-Hung

BUDDHIST REFORMER AND GREAT APOSTLE OF ETHICAL VEGETARIANISM
1565-1615

Some 17 years after the death in the West of Leonardo Da Vinci, there was born on the other side of the earth, during the Ming Dynasty in the aging Middle Kingdom, a man who was to become one of the greatest apostles of vegetarianism and man's ethical obligation to the entire animal world ever known—namely, the great and much-to-be-revered Chu-hung* (1565-1615). He came on the scene when Buddhism was at a very low ebb in China and very much in decline. One may even surmise that a certain laxness in regard to the maintenance of a strictly vegetarian diet had penetrated Chinese Buddhism from the Theravadin lands to the south.

Inspired by the dedicated personality and multifaceted endeavours of Chu-hung, Buddhism in China took on new life and became a vibrant, living force in Chinese society, despite its minority status. Chu-hung achieved such a phenomenon by diverse means. Firstly, he tirelessly campaigned for the observance of a strictly vegetarian diet combined with an actively compassionate treatment of animals as basic to Buddhist ethic. Secondly, he sought to promote a Buddhist lay movement among all stratas of Chinese society. Indeed, more than any other single figure, Chu-hung was responsible for the widespread growth "lay Buddhism" and the formation of "Buddhist Lay Societies" throughout China.

A monk himself, Chu-hung saw the necessity of making Buddhism more accessible to laymen in order to increase its influence

---

* For a study of Chu-hung see *The Revival of Buddhism in China* by Chun-fang Yu. Columbia University Press. New York, 1981.

within Chinese life. Thus, he saw his "mission" as one of promoting Buddhism and Buddhist ethic among people living active lives within Chinese society, house-holders and families with ordinary worldly interests and concerns—from farmers and tradesmen to wealthy merchants, aristocrats, and the scholarly elite. His goal was to broaden their essentially Confucian sense of ethic to include a compassionate sensitivity towards the animal world and inculcate in them a rigorous sense of karma—both in terms of karmic retribution for the taking of animal life and the acquisition of karmic merit through compassionate action or non-action.

The acquisition of merit, taught the revered Chu-hung, was a simple matter. While venerating the Buddhas and Bodhisattvas, one simply applied in one's life the quality of Compassion to every action or non-action in regard to both one's fellow men and to all animal beings, even the least, which is to say, insects. Naturally, this involved following a strictly vegetarian diet, which he declared— perhaps as a "skillful means" of inducement—resulted *in itself* in the acquisition of merit. Such merit, he held, would not only cancel out one's own negative karma, but could be applied as well, through transference, to the dead and to the negation of the evil karma which they had acquired. Hence, Chu-hung's emphasis on "Vegetarian Banquets for the Dead," which he promoted everywhere as a major aspect of "filial piety."

Buddhist vegetarian banquets ("ch'ia" in Chinese) were, of course, nothing new in China. They were (and are) held on various Buddhist festivals and holy days commemorating not only the chief events in the life of the Gautama Buddha, Shakyamuni, but also the feast days of other Buddhas and Bodhisattvas as well as certain monk "saints" connected with some particular sect, temple, or locality. They were also widely held on the anniverseries of the ritual consecration of particular temples, and to commemorate the dead.

Chu-hung simply emphasized the importance of the vegetarian feasts commemorating the dead as something to be carried out not only at the temples, but in the homes of Buddhist householders everywhere, on behalf of dead relatives and friends every time an anniversary occurred. What is more, he encouraged the attendance at such vegetarian feasts of non-Buddhists so that they might become acquainted with Buddhist ethic and at the same time be exposed to a wide variety of delectable vegetarian dishes! Thus, he manifest to all that Buddhism need not be unduly monastic and ascetic. In other words, a process of "sinification," which had begun in Chinese Buddhism centuries before, reached its full development in Chu-hung through whose efforts it became fully assimilated into busy, gregarious Chinese family life with its love of banquets and appreciation of culinary art—all within the strict confines of a Buddhist ethic which proscribed the taking of animal life and the use of animals for "food" or "medicine."

In his Commentary on the Bodhisattva Precepts contained in *The Sutra of Brahma's Net*, Chu-hung emphasized the observance of a vegetarian diet as essential in fulfilling the primary Buddhist precept of not killing or harming sentient beings. At the same time, he connected vegetarian observance with filial piety and fulfilling one's duties to the dead. To the end of promoting the observance of the first precept, Chu-hung and his followers, both monastic and lay, frequently went forth to exhort fishermen, hunters, butchers, and those who raised animals for eating to cease and desist their evil practices, for their own sakes as well as for those of their victims. Nor was he uncaring about the predicaments faced by such persons when they ceased to be involved in the killing of animals. He and other persons within the Buddhist community helped them in acquiring other jobs and entering other lines of work.

To simply refrain from harming animals was not enough for Chu-hung. He urged his followers *to actively manifest Compassion* towards them, even going out of their way to do so. Thus, he extolled as a necessary practice, imperative on all devout Buddhists, "The Release of Life," by which he signified the purchase and release of animals which had been intended "for the table." To quote Chun-fang Yu: "The motivations for performing such acts were rooted not in mere ethical demands, but had deep religious and psychological roots. When a person killed another sentient being, he broke the hidden bonds among all forms of life. Violence alienated the violator not only from . . . cosmic harmony, but also, ultimately, from himself."[46] On the other hand, each time the observant Buddhist released a creature from impending death, and returned it to freedom, "he reaffirmed the original bond among all sentient beings."[47]

A major activity in this respect was the purchase of tortoises, fish, birds, and mammals which had been intended for the table— and freeing them in elaborate "Life-Releasing" ceremonies, presided over by Buddhist monks. Chu-hung indeed regarded the release of a tortoise as one of most meritorious acts possible to man as tortoises had been known to save the lives of drowning men at sea!

Chu-hung's essays, *To Refrain from Killing* and *On Releasing Sentient Beings* are said by author Chun-fang Yu to be classics of their genre. These writings, in fact, led to a vogue among Chinese Buddhist lay people to form "Societies for the Release of Life" or "Fangsheng Hui." Such associations collected funds to purchase animals, as well as, in some cases, to maintain them. The members also built, by means of their own labour, "Ponds for the Release of Life" where fresh water fish, obtained from fishermen, could be freed. In certain cases where it was felt that the "water brethren" were in possible danger from human predators, members of the societies were appointed to keep watch for their safety. The ideal location for such ponds was seen as being within the enclosed walls of open-roofed ruined temples and, whenever possible, such sites were chosen as preferred locations of the "Ponds for the Release of Life."

The members of these societies also provided free vegetarian meals for the poor, thus revealing the extensiveness to which Chuhung's Movement provided remedies for various social problems. It also aimed at bringing about Buddhist unity, attempting to bring together different Buddhist schools in a kind of synthesis of Pure Land, Ch'an, and Tien'tai teachings—although Pure Land remained the dominant element.

It is not without interest that the revered Chu-hung and his teachings came to the notice of the Jesuit, Matteo Ricci, who came to China in 1582 and succeeded in converting many Chinese to Christianity. Ricci, in fact, with typical Christian intolerance, initiated a deep-rooted controversy between Buddhism and Christianity, a controversy which manifest quite clearly the irreconcilable differences between the two religions.

Taking the usual Christian position that, like vegetables and the fruits of the earth, animals were created for man's "use and benefit," to do with whatever he chose, Ricci launched into a vigorous attack against the basic Buddhist precept of not harming or hurting animal beings. In this, he particularly condemned Chuhung's pivotal foundation for the Lay Buddhist Movement—Compassion for Life—as well as the observance of vegetarianism and the active manifestation of Compassion in "The Release of Life," terming such phenomena "absurd." He also, on a very exoteric level, condemned the theory of "reincarnation," a matter which need not concern us here.

12. The Revival of Vegetarianism in the West— Early Awakenings in England

16TH-18TH CENTURY

It was in England, a land long noted for its decided emphasis on a carnivorous diet, that both vegetarianism and a sense of ethical obligation towards the animal world were manifest for the first time in the West *as widespread movements* since the gradual demise of the ancient Greco-Roman civilization.

It may be noted that at least some followers of the vegetarian tradition in Greco-Roman Paganism must have been present in Britain during the period between 43 A.D. and the 5th century when England was a Roman Colony. The existence of a dedication verse[48] in honour of the Empress Julia Domna at a shrine to Juno Caelestis at Cavoran indicates the probability of such. As the reader will recall from the section on Apollonius of Tyana in Chapter 6, Julia Domna (d. 217 A.D.) was the patroness of Philostratus whom she commissioned to compile a life of Apollonius of Tyana—a leading propagator of Pythagorean vegetarianism and fervent opponent of blood sacrifice.

Among the first individuals to play a part, however small and perhaps even inadvertent, in the "modern" British vegetarian awakening was the notable Humanist, Sir Thomas More (1477-1535). Although there is no evidence that More was actually a vegetarian himself (this would have been a nearly supernatural feat in Henry VIII's England), he nevertheless condemned the barbarity of the hunt and, *for whatever it is worth*, in his *Utopia*, depicted the "highest rung" of his utopian society as abstainers from the flesh of animals. Whether or not one may regard this as an indication that More at least held the vegetarian way of life to be a desirable ideal depends on how one views this curious and often puzzling piece of fiction—a matter concerning which there is no absolute agreement.

He did, however, at least bring the phenomenon of vegetarianism as a dietary alternative to the attention of the reading public at a time when it was virtually non-existent. If a vegetarian movement had, in fact, come into being during More's lifetime, in all probability he would have been among its most fervent supporters.

In any case, during the 17th and 18th centuries which followed, the observance of a vegetarian diet gradually increased as did a sense of man's relationship to the animal world and the place of both in Nature. John Ray, a 17th century naturalist, theorized that mankind was by nature, herbivorous, rather than carnivorous. Furthermore, according to Mennel,[49] as early as 1650, various individuals in Britain had adopted a vegetarian diet and, in 1683, a book advocating vegetarianism was published in London. Its title was *The Way to Health* and its author was one Thomas Tryon.

One of the first persons prominent in British life and cultural circles to unequivocally express vegetarian sentiments. was none other than the renowned Alexander Pope (1688-1744), poet and leading Classical Greek and Latin scholar. Pope's translations of Homer's Illiad (1715) and Odyssey (1744) as well as of other Classical writers are still read today. Not only did Pope play a leading role in the 18th century Greco-Roman Revival, but he derived much of the inspiration for his own ethics and world view from that great apostle of vegetarianism, Plutarch, whose influence on the vegetarian movement of pre-Victorian and Victorian England cannot be overestimated.

Pope praises the exceptionally good nature of "the excellent Plutarch" and, time and again, quotes the latter on man's ethical obligation to treat animals in a kindly and beneficent manner.[50] "It is no more than the obligation of our very birth," states Pope, quoting Plutarch from his *Life of Cato*, "to practice equity to our own kind, but humanity may be extended through the whole order of creatures, even to the meanest . . . on all below us."[51]

In an article published in *The Guardian*[52] on May 21, 1713, Pope presents his views on the ethical treatment of animals so strongly and with such passion that it is obvious that he himself *must have been, indeed can only have been a vegetarian*— although as far as we are aware, no precise evidence exists concerning the matter. Inasmuch as Alexander Pope was a Roman Catholic, he may have felt compelled to keep his actual observance of ethical vegetarianism strictly private.

In the above-mentioned article, Pope not only condemns the "wantoness" and "ignorant barbarity" involved in the killing and hunting of animals, but speaks of man's moral obligation "to relieve and assist" all animals "in their wants and distresses," mentioning "their cries and voices" as "intended to move our pity." He then proceeds to condemn the human savagery and monstrous cruelty involved in boiling lobsters alive, whipping pigs to death, and other dreadful tortures to which animals are subjected as sacrifices to human gluttony. But, as he points out, man receives a just reward for his gluttonous savagery in the diseases and ill health which it brings with it. He speaks, too, of the horror which he experiences at beholding "kitchens covered with blood" and "bestrued with the scattered heads and mangled limbs of those who were slain."[53]

There can be no question that Alexander Pope played a not insignificant role in the awakening of the British conscience in regard to the weal of the animal world and the coming into existence of the vegetarian movement in Great Britain.

The medical profession of the time, too, was not without advocates of a vegetarian diet. Among those doctors promoting the latter from the perspective of health and nutrition was one of the outstanding physicians of the era, the well-known George Cheyne (1671-1743) who was a native of Aberdeenshire, Scotland. Not only was Cheyne a prominent doctor, he was also a leading member of the Royal Society. Regarding the eating of animals as a leading cause of illness and disease, he nevertheless favoured the use of milk and milk products in conjunction with a wide range of vegetarian foods. He also utilized *particular* vegetables and fruits in the treatment of *specific* diseases.

Cheyne[54] is said to have met with considerable success both in promoting a vegetarian diet and curing his patients by means of abstinence from animal flesh, even among the "genteel epicures" of Bath who comprised an important element of his practice.

No less important than Cheyne as a medical figure who advocated a vegetarian diet was the eminent Italian doctor, Antonio Cocci (1695-1758), a professor of medicine and philosophy at the University of Firenze. Seldom mentioned today, Cocci is a major neglected figure in the revival of the Classical Greco-Roman vegetarian tradition. In his work, entitled *The Pythagorean Diet*, which was published in Firenze (Florence) in 1743, Cocci emphasizes the necessity of excluding animal flesh from one's diet *for reasons of both health and ethics,* hailing Pythagoras as "The Great Physician" who sought to improve not only the health, but also the morals of mankind.

Although influencing a few of his fellow countrymen sufficiently to adopt a vegetarian diet, Cocci's book met with its greatest successes and bore its greatest fruits abroad, particularly in England where in 1745 an English translation was printed by R. Dodsley in London. Quite aside from the increasing interest among the English in health and diet, the very fact that Cocci's book dealt with Pythagoras and his philosophy insured its popularity—at least in literary and academic circles as well as among the educated upper classes in general, for whom an interest in the Classical Ancient World represented something "fashionable" and avant garde.

Also contributing to the development of a frame of mind leading to a vegetarian perspective, although in a quite different way and less directly than Alexander Pope, George Cheyne, and Antonio Cocci was Jeremy Bentham (1718-1832). A scholar and jurist who was prominent in British affairs during the second half of the 1700s, Bentham not only believed that all animals should be treated in a kindly fashion, but insisted that it was man's moral obligation to do so. He looked to an ideal society in the future (still not realized!) wherein all cruelty to animals (including hunting, butchering, and cruel misuse) would be strictly proscribed as "crimes." Given his views, it is more than likely that Bentham followed a vegetarian diet.

Among those 18th century individuals who advocated an ethically-oriented vegetarianism in the British Isles was a certain John Oswald of Edinburgh, who was, in fact, very much of a vegetarian activist. Devoting himself to promoting an ethical perspective which included opposition to all man-inflicted animal suffering, Oswald tirelessly travelled throughout England and Scotland, giving lectures to promote an ethically-based vegetarian diet as well as compassionate behaviour towards all members of the animal world.

Although a self-proclaimed atheist, Oswald, who had served in the British Army in India, nevertheless, to some degree derived his philosophy and ethic of vegetarianism from his study of the religions of India in which he possessed considerable interest. His book, *The Cry of Nature or An Appeal to Mercy and Justice on Behalf of the Persecuted Animals* was published in London in 1791.

Very different in orientation from the various vegetarian perspectives mentioned above was that advocated by certain small obscure Christian sects, such as that of William Cowherd, which came into existence in the late 18th and early 19th centuries. In nearly all such cases, the vegetarian diet which these sects required of their members was quite lacking in any ethical basis and had nothing to do with any sense of moral obligation to the animal world. Although in some cases, health and disease prevention did to some degree enter the picture, ascetic self-denial as well as "clean living" and a sense of animals being "unclean" were the reasons for their maintaining a vegetarian diet. Most of these sects were short-lived, although others survived for a longer period of time. Inasmuch as these small religious movements were basically Christian in orientaion, however non-traditional, they were notably out of step with the majority of British vegetarians of the period who were of a predominently non-Christian cast of mind.

13. The Development of British Vegetarianism During the 19th and 20th Centuries

THE CULTURAL-HISTORICAL BACKGROUND, CONTRIBUTING FACTORS, AND LEADING PERSONALITIES

Although the stage was set in the 18th century for the spread of vegetarianism in Britain, it was only during the 19th century that vegetarianism became widespread as a way of life and an organized movement.

In 1802, Joseph Ritson's *Essay on the Abstinence From Animal Food* was published. Ritson, a barrister and an outspoken atheist, actively campaigned throughout Great Britain for the kindly treatment of animals and the "ethical necessity" of adopting a vegetarian diet. He viewed the eating of animals as an appalling act of barbarism which had no place in a civilized society. Together with his publisher, Richard Philips, and the printer, George Nicolson, Ritson formed a nucleus for the active propagation of vegetarianism in Great Britain. All three of these individuals sought to advance vegetarianism in conjunction with an awakening social consciousness which involved a deep-rooted concern for the suffering of sentient beings, both human and animal.

Some 8 years after the publication of Ritson's appeal, yet another call to vegetarianism appeared, this being John Newton's work, *A Return to Nature or a Defense of the Vegetable Regimen* which was published in London by Cadell in 1810. In it, the author urged all to adopt a totally herbivorous diet as the only one sanctioned by Nature. Like all of the 19th century English books on vegetarianism, most of which enjoyed a wide circulation in their day, this tome is extremely rare today. In all such writings, the groundwork was being laid for the advancement and increase of vegetarian practice as well as a change in attitude and perspective, involving both ethics and health. As the 19th century unfolded, the

old England of Henry VIII and the Elizabethans with its vast consumption of animal flesh increasingly gave the appearance of having been very much tempered by saner dietary perspectives with an
ever-larger number of people observing the ancient "Pythagorean
diet." Many diverse aspects of the cultural and intellectual life of the
times contributed to this phenomenon.

First and foremost, one may cite the revival of interest in the
ancient Classical World of Greece and Rome—its literature, philosophy, ethic, history, art, and architecture. Not unconnected with
this interest was the rapid development of archeological science
with its extensive excavations as well as the fact that styles and
fashions in furniture and china together with the aesthetic motifs
utilized in various objects ranging from clocks to tomb memorials
took on decided Greco-Roman features.

Intellectually and aesthetically, winds of change permeated
the atmosphere of the British Isles during the second half of the
1700s and throughout much of the 1800s. It was a time of mental
and spiritual ferment which was to continue at an ever-accelerating
pace well into the present century; it was also a time which involved the birth of many new ideas or, in some cases, the rebirth of certain very ancient ones. A re-orientation occurred concerning many aspects of life, thus challenging various assumptions
which hitherto had prevented the formulation of new perspectives
and approaches. There was an increasing revulsion towards the
violation and exploitation of sentient beings, both human and animal. In 1807, for example, England had made the slave trade illegal.

New ideas and ideals came to the fore as well as a revival of
older ones, notably those based upon *the best* of Classical Greece
and Rome. Among these ideas and ideals was vegetarianism. Indeed, the existence of a vegetarian ethic in the ancient Greco-
Roman world was a subject which could scarcely be avoided after
the "re-discovery" of western man's Greco-Roman heritage, particularly that deriving from Pythagoras, Empedocles, Theophrastes,
Ovid, Plutarch, and Porphyry. Even the historian Lecky notes
Plutarch's concern with man's ethical obligation to the animal
world.

To a large degree, this revival of the vegetarian ethic and philosophy of the ancient world was in conjunction with a rejection of
Christianity and what was seen as its distorted sense of ethic. The
revival of the vegetarian way of life in the West also took place

within the context of an increasing sensitivity to the aesthetic, particularly in relation to everyday life. Not to be overlooked in this whole process was a deepening of an intuitive "Pantheistic" sensitivity to Nature and a sense of man's kinship with the animal world. In such remarkable paintings as George Stubb's portrait of a monkey, painted in 1798, one could not escape the feeling of profound empathy with the subject as well as an awareness of mutually-felt emotions. All of these matters were involved in a coming to the fore of a deeply-rooted sense of moral obligation to both one's fellow man and to the animal world—in other words, a general ethical concern for the weal of sentient beings.

THE ROLE OF PERCY BYSSHE SHELLEY

The importance of Percy Bysshe Shelley (1792-1822)—poet, eccentric, "romantic," aesthete, traveller, and humanist philosopher—for the development of the vegetarian movement and the formation of its rationale in Great Britain can scarcely be overestimated. While his writings advocating a vegetarian diet (see his *Essay on the Vegetable System of Diet* and his *Vindication of Natural Diet*)[55] were hardly the first to be published in Britain, Shelley's reputation as a poet, aesthete, and leading Humanist of his generation, as well as his position in society, assured him of a different and perhaps somewhat more "avant garde" readership and influence than those advocates of vegetarian diet immediately preceding him.

There can be no doubt that Shelley's essays as well as the ideals and causes which he espoused proved to be immensely influential within a certain literary, aesthetic, intellectual milleu both during his lifetime and long after his death. An idealized Shelley had even become the object of a minor "cult" by the time of his centenary in 1892.

Shelley was convinced that the eating of animals was not only an act which was unnatural, but also a major factor contributing to the diverse diseases effecting the human organism. He equated such behaviour with both barbarism and irrationality. Indeed, he, like Pythagoras, saw the killing and eating of animals as a "derangement" of the natural harmony of Nature and earthly life. He spoke of man's "contaminating dominion over the animal world" and of humankind's "unnatural craving for dead flesh."[56]

Comparing the slaughter of innocent animals to the dreadful carnage and irrationality of wars, Shelley writes: "So far as just philosophy and natural sentiments shall prevail among mankind, so far am I persuaded that the practice of destroying and devouring animals will come to be contemplated in the light of an unnatural and pernicious outrage."[57] Thus, it may be seen that Shelley's vegetarianism was not an isolated phenomenon, but existed within the fuller context of his ethical sensitivity and general Humanist perspective which included opposition to the irrationality and barbarity of war (this at a time when much of Europe had been devastated in Napoleon's wars of conquest) as well as all manner of injustice, exploitation, and oppression of one people or segment of society by another. Religiously, Shelley was decidedly anti-Christian. His world view may be variously described as essentially atheist or, at times, vaguely pantheist—in either case, within the context of an enlightened Humanist ethic.

Shelley and his lady, Harriet Westbrook, ceased eating animals in March 1812, while living in Dublin. A few months later, they met the vegetarian activist, John Newton, the author of *A Return to Nature or a Defence of the Vegetable Regimen*. Thus, Shelley became a member of Newton's vegetarian circle which included such eminent vegetarians as the previously mentioned Joseph Ritson— author, barrister, and outspoken atheist—and Dr. William Lambe, a prominent doctor, who, like George Cheyne in the previous century, advocated a strictly vegetarian diet as both a cure and preventitive for numerous ailments. The presence of Shelley in Newton's circle drew an ever-increasing number of people into a vegetarian-oriented perspective. Not only were most of these, well-educated individuals with a highly refined aesthetic sense, but they were also persons who were essentially alienated from Christianity. Nearly all were "freethinkers," atheists, or pantheists.

Shelley, for inspiration looked back to the "Golden Age"* in man's distant past which, as we have seen, was viewed as a time when a higher ethic prevailed and man did not take the lives of animals or indulge in sadistic cruelty towards them or towards his fellow man in irrational and barbaric warfare; a time when the human diet was limited to vegetables, fruits, grains, herbs, and nuts.

* See Chapter 1 as well as Chapter 9 for the "Golden Age."

Shelley believed, too, that the "Golden Age" would inevitably recur at some future date. "The Coming Age," he wrote, "is shadowed on the past as on a glass" (Ahasuerus, the Wandering Jew in Shelley's *Hellas*).

For Shelley, as for all vegetarians, the very sight of dead flesh, with "its bloody juices and raw horror" excited "intolerable loathing and disgust."[58] His particular mode of eating, however, neither was nor is common to all vegetarians. Shelley's tastes in food were very simple, his mode of eating decidedly "ascetic," although such could scarcely be said of the aesthetic and sexual aspects of his personality. Shelley was no monk. It may be assumed, however, that he would have looked with distaste on George Bernard Shaw's penchant for gourmet vegetarian fare a century later. Shelley often ate plain boiled potatoes and "pease porridge." He was particularly fond of *raw* vegetables and fruits. Turnips, lettuce, apples, pears, oranges, and gooseberries were among his favorites. All were consumed with utmost simplicity. One gathers that he disapproved not only of elaborate culinary preparation, but of spices as well! Many English vegetarians, however, particularly as the century advanced, took a great delight in the preparation of gourmet vegetarian meals. This serves to illustrate the extreme diversity that exists among vegetarian life styles.

Rather ironically, in view of his own brevity of life, Shelley had a certain fascination with longevity. Indeed, he viewed living to an advanced age as one of the advantages of a vegetarian diet, noting that several long-lived British eccentrics of the past had confined themselves to strictly vegetarian fare. These individuals include one "Old Parr" who reached the astonishing age of 152 years (!) and a Mary Patten who lived to be 136. Any further information concerning them seems to be lost in obscurity.

For Shelley, as for many others involved in the vegetarian revival of the last century, Pythagoras, the apostle of western vegetarianism who lived over 2,000 years before, remained a major inspiration. Like Pythagoras, Shelley made a point of being kind to animals and even insects. He also engaged in varied deeds of kindness and charity among the ill and poor living near him. In obvious imitation of Pythagoras (and unknown to him, of Chinese Buddhists), he not infrequently purchased still living crayfish from fish vendors and returned them to "their lurking places in the Thames."[59]

Plutarch, too, was a major inspiration among British vegetarians of Shelley's day, many of whom were capable of reading his exhortation to the vegetarian way of life in the original Latin. Shelley, in fact, translated this essay into English and planned a preface to it. Rather curiously and for reasons unknown, the translation was never published. It is interesting to note that Shelley sought to promote his vegetarian ideals by means of his poetry which was not unpopular throughout the British Isles. Thus, his *A Vindication of Natural Diet* was first presented as a footnote to his poem *Queen Mab*, only later being published as a separate pamphlet. Not to be overlooked as an expression of Shelley's vegetarianism and love of the animal world are the sentiments contained in his poem *Laon and Cyntha*. In this, "the Great Festival of the Nations" is represented as a "Bloodless Banquet" at which both birds and beasts proclaim that never again shall their blood stain a human feast.

BRITISH VEGETARIANISM AFTER SHELLEY— CONTRIBUTING FACTORS AND THE CULTURAL-HISTORICAL BACKGROUND

As the 19th century advanced, the British vegetarian movement became stronger and stronger. Although many of its adherents held views almost identical with those of Shelley, others observed a vegetarian diet for medical or nutritional reasons only. There were also those whose vegetarianism was in conjunction with the teachings of some particular religious sect.

Finally, in the second half of the 1840's, vegetarian societies began springing up throughout Britain, particularly in the larger urban centres. It was only around this time that the words "vegetarian" and "vegetarianism" began to be used. Until then, a mode of eating which excluded animal flesh was simply termed "the Pythagorean diet," "the natural diet," or "the vegetable regimen." Via Shelley, the words "bloodless banquets" were also sometimes used to describe vegetarian meals.

In a round about way, even the Industrial Revolution may be viewed as a factor which contributed to the development of British vegetarianism, inasmuch as the plight of industrial factory workers eventually awakened general humanitarian concerns in regard to both men and animals. These included an awareness of the need to improve the terrible conditions to which the inmates of prisons and mental institutions as well as the urban poor were subjected. In this general awakening of the human conscience, concern was also manifest for the abused and suffering members of the animal kingdom. The result was the formation of various "animal protection" societies. The "Humane Movement" itself, however, contributed only peripherally to the growth of British vegetarianism. Rather curiously, most participants in this movement did not feel that it was ethically obligatory to follow a vegetarian diet. Among those few who felt differently concerning this matter was the well-known Jewish philanthropist, Lewis Gompertz (d. 1861). A dedicated vegetarian who abstained from all flesh foods, Gompertz also excluded dairy products and eggs from his diet. He is of interest as one of the earlier advocates of a Jewish vegetarianism. His Jewish faith, his interest in Pythagorean philosophy, and his insistence on the observance of a strictly vegetarian diet all seem to have aroused the wrath of many non-vegetarians involved in the so-called "Animal Protection Movement." Indeed, one cannot but be astonished that the animal welfare and protection movement in its various guises— which ranged from from opposition to the cruelties suffered by animals in laboratory experiments and in "blood sports" to their exploitation as work animals—did not, at least eventually, become wholly vegetarian in its orientation. Unfortunately, this was not the case. The greatest anomaly of all was that while slaughterhouse cruelties were protested, only rarely did this involve any sense of meat eating itself as ethically unacceptable!

Ultimately, most of the animal welfare organizations served as little more than emotional pacifiers to assuage an awakening conscience in regard to animal suffering without going to what many viewed as "the extreme of vegetarianism." Indeed, it was a rare event for a participant in the movement to venture beyond the threshold of "respectability" to vegetarianism. The very wealthy as well as those of some cultural status, like Shelley himself at the beginning of the century or Gompertz in the middle of the century could, of course, do so, but not without offending the "propriety" of the more conventional elements of the middle class whose "animal welfare" associations not infrequently degenerated into little more than dog fancier's clubs.

As for the early "conservationists," most were poles apart from the vegetarian ethic, and not a few were of the Theodore

Roosevelt ilk—hunters who thought in terms of "game preserves!"
An exception was Yorkshire vicar, Francis Morris, with his laudible
work for wild bird protection during the 1870s. Needless to
say, the usual conservationist idea of "preserving an endangered
species" is hardly the same thing as the bird-loving vegetarian's
keenly felt perception that every individual bird has "a right to
life!"

Among the phenomena which contributed to the development of the vegetarian perspective may be mentioned Darwinism
and its deeply felt sense of man's kinship with the animal world.
The old barriers created by Christian theology were breaking down;
Nature and the animal world were no longer seen as beneath or
below man, and consequently were less and less viewed as appropriate "objects" for human exploitation. Indeed, in poets such as
Wordsworth and Swinbourne a romanticized pantheistic sense of
Nature evolved which led to the idea that animals are to be respected and loved by man rather than hunted, slaughtered, and
eaten!

By the 1880s, the Vegetarian Movement in Great Britain had
very firmly taken root, its advocates including persons of extremely
diverse perspectives, if not backgrounds. Most were well-educated,
highly cultured individuals of considerable refinement. Many could
be characterized as "naturists" and aesthetes. They included aca-
demics, persons involved in literature and the arts, and not a few
social-conscious Humanists whose concerns were, above all, with
"social reform." Politically, they ranged from conservative Tory
monarchists to Fabian Socialists (also, incidently, mostly monarchists). In many respects, what they represented had been antici-
pated some 60 years before in Percy Bysshe Shelley and his circle.

Religiously, they ranged from atheists, agnostics, and pantheists to Theosophists, members of the Vedanta Society, and the adherents of other newly-formed religious groups of an essentially
Hindu orientation. Christians involved in the British Vegetarian
Movement of the late 19th century were few and far between.
Those few who were, ranged from the ocassional eccentric Church
of England vicar to the followers of small newly-devised Christian
sects or schools of thought, such as that of Anna Kingsford. Due to
Papal opposition to the idea that man has a moral duty to treat
animals in a kindly and compassionate manner, Roman Catholics,
as such, were quite lacking. After all, Pope Pius IX had recently

refused to permit the establishment of a society concerned with preventing cruelty to animals in the city of Rome on the grounds that it would imply an ethical obligation to the animal world on the part of man![60]

The specific form which vegetarianism took among its adherents during that period differed widely. Some ate only raw vegetables and fruits while others made every vegetarian meal a veritable gourmet feast which involved elaborate culinary preparation. While some eschewed all dairy products, others utilized diverse cheeses (made without rennet, which is an animal derivative) and other milk products as an important element in their diets.

Some leading vegetarians, such as Dr. Allinson, an early advocate of prophilactics and birth control, promoted vegetarianism in conjunction with a broader program of good health and "simple living," which was seen as involving fresh air, exercise, and living "close to Nature." Other vegetarians were quite indifferent to such matters, being solely concerned with vegetarianism as an ethical obligation.

Interestingly enough, too, while the British "Raj" in India resulted in considerable western influence in native life and culture for better or sometimes for worse, it also facilitated a flow of Indian influence into English life on both internal and external levels. By the 80s, natives of India were not only coming to Britain to pursue higher education in British universities, but many were also emigrating to various British urban centres where they opened shops, import businesses, and restaurants.

Indeed, there can be no doubt that the popularization of Indian cuisine and foods among the English contributed not a little to the Vegetarian Movement, for through exposure to them, people were able to see how varied, delectable, and reasonably-priced vegetarian foods could be. Persons who had served in the British Army in India also played a part in popularizing Indian foods in Britain, as when they returned to England after years of service in India, they often brought with them a taste for the foods and condiments of India. While East Indian restaurants, with their chiefly vegetarian menus, were coming into existence in Britain's larger cities between 1880 and 1915, so too were non-Indian vegetarian restaurants, the fares of which varied from extremely plain to gourmet. Being a vegetarian in Britain was becoming much less difficult than it had been.

Not unimportant in the momentum gathered by the Vegetarian Movement in late Victorian England was a book by one Howard Williams entitled *The Ethics of Diet*, which was published in 1890. This volume was a defence of the vegetarian point of view, citing many of the great vegetarians of the past. Unfortunately, the scarcity of this book today places it in the "rare book" category.

HENRY SALT AND EDWARD CARPENTER

A leading, although today seldom-mentioned, figure in the development of the Vegetarian Movement in Victorian and post-Victorian England was Henry Salt (1851-1939). A one-time Master of Eton, Henry Salt, who was something of a "naturist," resigned his professorship in order to live close to Nature in the "wilds of Surrey."

Salt was a man who possessed a remarkable empathy with both animals in all their diversity and with the suffering and exploited clements of human society. He believed in "making friends" with animals; he viewed them as independent beings, entitled to be treated with respect and kindness.

Salt's philosophy of vegetarianism is clearly set forth in both his *Plea For Vegetarianism* published in 1886 and in his *Seventy Years Among the Savages*, which was printed by Allen and Unwin in 1921. He saw vegetarianism as an ethical obligation and considered himself a vegetarian in the Shelley tradition. Notably anti-Christian, he was openly scornful of many of the customs and conventions prevalent in Christian society. Speaking of his own adoption of a vegetarian diet, he says: "I then found myself realizing, with an amazement which time has not diminished, that the 'meat' which . . . I was accustomed to regard—like bread, or fruit, or vegetables—as a mere commodity of the table, was, in truth dead flesh, the actual flesh and blood of oxen, sheep, swine, and other animals that are slaughtered in vast numbers under conditions so horrible that even to mention the subject at our dinner tables is an unpardonable offense . . .

Now when I began to put questions to my friends and acquaintances about this apparently glaring inconsistency of our 'civilization,' I could not help observing . . . that the answers by which they sought to parry my awkward importunities were extremely

evasive and sophistical, reminding me of the quibbling explana-
tions which travellers have received from cannibals when they in-
quired too closely into certain dietary observances."[61]

He speaks also of "animals habitually tortured for sport, science, and the table;" he condemned unequivocally the "organized
butchery" of hunters, among whom "every contemptable manner of
cowardly slaughter is practiced as 'sportsmanlike' and 'manly.'"[62]
Perhaps, continues Salt on the following page, in view of man's
"insatiable blood lust" and "penchant for eating animal corpses," we
should be "grateful that they (the eaters of animals) have not eaten
us (the vegetarians)!"

Henry Salt saw vegetarianism as an ethical obligation. He also
viewed it as one "reform" among many necessary for a new Humanist world. Along with his advocacy of a vegetarian diet, his
respect for the animal world, and his emphasis on the need for man
to live in harmony with the world of Nature, Salt also strongly endorsed the still-suspect ideas of general sexual emancipation and
the use of condoms as a means of birth control. He stood for a new
Humanist society which rejected many of the uncritically-accepted
mores and conventions of the times.

Not to be overlooked for his contribution to the British vegetarianism of this period is Edward Carpenter (1844-1929). A friend
of Henry Salt, Carpenter was an activist in nearly all fields of social
reform. At one time an Anglican priest, he relinquished "holy orders" in 1874 in order to champion a number of liberal social
causes. These included not only vegetarianism, but also feminism,
Fabian Socialism, prison reform, anti-pollution legislation, nudism,
and "sexual freedom." Walt Whitman was one of his favourite au-
thors. His pamphlet, *Homogenic Love*, published in 1895, was one
of the earliest defences of homosexuality as a legitimate natural
preference. Viewed as something of an "eccentric" in his day, Edward Carpenter* unquestionably played a leading role in the formation of a new perspective which was not only more tolerant of
human diversity but sought to implement a new sense of ethic
which involved many very avant-garde ideals concerning both

---

* For further information on Carpenter, the reader is directed to *Victorian Britain—
An Encyclopedia.* Sally Mitchell, editor. Garland Pub., London and New York, 1988.
Also see C. Tsuzuki's study, *Edward Carpenter, Prophet of Human Fellowship* as
indicated in the Bibliography.

humankind and animals—ideals involving an active tolerance, compassion, and non-violence which remain unrealized in human society even today.

GEORGE BERNARD SHAW

Another quite different but no less eccentric personality of major importance in British vegetarianism was playwrite George Bernard Shaw (1856-1952). Indeed, the very name of this often cantankerous, frequently cynical, and notably outspoken literary gentleman became, for many, synomymous with vegetarianism. In some respects, this identification in the mind of the general public created some erroneous impressions. Shaw, for instance, frequently condemned "the carnivorous diet" in the same breath that he condemned tea, coffee, and all forms of alcohol. For perhaps the majority of vegetarians, partaking of such beverages is a matter of ethical indifference and personal preference, having nothing whatever to do with with vegetarianism as such. Tolstoy, for example, who excluded both meat and alcohol from his diet, drank enormous quantities of tea. Other vegetarians, both in the past and in the contemporary world, particularly those of gourmet tendencies, by no means exclude fine quality wines from their diets. Others enjoy fine herbal liquers such as Green Chartreuse, and still others consume moderate quantities of beer or ale. *None of these beverages, after all, involve the taking of animal life!* Whether or not one partakes of them is entirely a matter of personal preference, *not of ethics.*

As with so many British vegetarians, Shaw's adoption of a vegetarian diet in the early 80s of the last century occurred through the lingering influence of Shelley and his Humanist philosophy. Like Shelley, Shaw believed that vegetarianism was among the various reforms needed to implement the coming into existence of a reasonably humane or ideal society. Also like Shelley, he was of the opinion that such a society could only come into being in conjunction with a well-reasoned opposition to Christianity and both the conventions of behaviour which it encouraged and its very much "wanting" or distorted sense of ethic—a recurrent theme among many western vegetarians. As Shaw stated at a Shelley Society meeting, he was proud to affirm that he, like Shelley, was not only an atheist, but also a vegetarian and a socialist.

Like many other British vegetarians of the time, such as the well-known journalist and early science fiction writer, H.G. Wells (1866-1946), Shaw was an active member of the London Fabian Society. This organization sought to bring into existence, by non-violent means, a socialist society dedicated to social justice and vastly improved conditions for the less fortunate elements of society, particularly factory workers and the urban poor. For Shaw and other vegetarians, who were by no means a majority within the Fabian Society, the addition of a vegetarian addenda to the organization's programme remained a much desired but unfulfilled goal. Shaw looked forward to the coming into being of a more humane and kindly society in which *both human and animal suffering* would be largely, if not altogether, eliminated. Closely associated with Shaw, and a good friend of his, Eton Master, J. L. Joynes, shared Shaw's vegetarian Humanist ideals.

Like the majority of vegetarians, both in his own time and in ours, Shaw's vegetarianism was based first and foremost on an empathy which he felt with the animal world. He sensed instinctively that a carnivorous diet is "an abomination." For him, meat-eating was quite simply and bluntly "cannibalism," an obnoxious form of conventional behaviour which needed to be overcome. He perceived each animal as an "individual personality" and he enjoyed talking to animals as "friends," hoping that they were as amused by him as he was by them.

Although Shaw noted that a vegetarian diet contributed to his mental and physical vitality, he possessed little or no interest in the health or nutritional aspect of such a diet. His vegetarianism was based, above all, on an abhorrence of being the cause, however indirectly, of animal suffering. He also experienced an extreme revulsion and disgust at the thought of eating the bodies of animals. He once said something to this effect concerning human carnivores—"Yes, they actually put them (dead animals) in their mouths, chew them up, and swallow them!" This statement unquestionably conveys something of the way most vegetarians feel about "meat eating."

Although Shaw shared Gandhi's and Tolstoy's dedication to vegetarian practice as well as their Humanist concerns for the correction of the diverse evils existent in human society, he was by no means in agreement with either their decidedly puritanical views concerning human sexuality or with their obsession with frugality and simplicity of fare. Shaw was fond of eating, and chose his food carefully. He liked among other things, thickly-buttered fine quality dark bread covered with red current jam, grapefruits (still something of a luxury in the Britain of his day), baked apples served with thick Devonshire cream, fancy puddings, spinach souffle, and numerous other dishes involving eggs and cheese. Indeed, his propensity for gourmet vegetarian dishes became greater and greater as he grew older.[63]

Although one can hardly count Shaw a *major* influence on British vegetarianism, neither can one neglect his part in it. As a very high-profile public figure, he certainly contributed to making vegetarianism known to the general public. Through identifying himself with it, Shaw also created in the mind of the public a certain connection between vegetarianism and "eccentricity." While such an identification could be misleading, the majority of vegetarians, then as today, tend to be persons who reject stereotyped modes of thought as well as ordinary conventional perspectives and approaches to human life and society. Indeed, as we have already noted, vegetarians over the centuries, in various historical circumstances, have generally represented the avant-garde of the day, the advanced thinkers and creative intellects of their times. They have been and are, for the most part, persons profoundly concerned with ethics as well as with social, and sometimes, political reform. Thus, in 19th and early 20th century Britain, the Vegetarian Movement developed very much in conjunction with a broader programme of Humanist social reforms.

What took place in Great Britain as well as elsewhere during the second half of the 19th century and well into the 20th century was a marvellous cross-fertilization of diverse ideas, philosophies, perspectives, and cultures—East and West. Out of this emerged a powerful Vegetarian Movement, a strengthening and extension of the Vegetarian Way of Life.

14. Gandhi—Bridge Between East and West

Mahatma Gandhi (1869-1948) affords us with an excellent illustration of the East-West cross-fertilization mentioned at the end of the previous chapter. Gandhi only became a *convinced* vegetarian in London, his Hindu vegetarian orientation until that time being more a matter of caste taboo than of ethic or philosophy. His intellectual or spiritual "conversion" to vegetarianism occurred only after he met the vegetarian activist and social reformer, Henry Salt and became familiar with Salt's views and writings. Also not unimportant in this process was his contact with the well-known poet and vegetarian, Sir Edwin Arnold (1833-1904), the author of *The Light of Asia*, a work inspired by the life and teachings of the Buddha. It was during his stay in England, too, that Gandhi became familiar with Howard William's *The Ethics of Diet*, a book which made a profound impression on him.

In the Bayswater District of London where he lived during his lengthy stay in England as a university student, Gandhi became involved in a "Vegetarian Club," himself serving as secretary. Other members included a Dr. Oldfield, who edited *The Vegetarian* magazine, as well as Sir Edwin Arnold. Later, Gandhi even served on the Executive Committee of the British Vegetarian Society.

It cannot be too strongly emphasized that Gandhi's whole philosophy of life with its ethics of non-violence and concern with the rectification of numerous social problems through the application of non-violence combined with social activism was not something that appeared out of nowhere, or something which Gandhi developed out of sources entirely Indian in origin. To the contrary, many different influences entered into it. It was, in fact, the result of *a fusion of various elements derived from both East and West*. In adapting western Humanist social concerns to the ancient Indian teaching of Ahimsa, Gandhi produced an ethic and philosophy of social change which was more powerful than either one was by itself.

Gandhi was profoundly impressed by Henry Salt's *Plea for Vegetarianism*, particularly the way in which Salt related vegetarian observance to the diverse aspects of social reform, thus placing it within a broader Humanist context. In England, Gandhi came to see vegetarianism as a matter of "common sense," particularly in regard to nutrition and disease prevention. Traditional Hindu dietary taboos had no such concerns. Rather than viewing a vegetarian diet simply as a "given" restriction to insure "ritual purity," Gandhi came to see it terms of "food reform" and ethics, as something to be observed by the whole of human society and not simply one or two of its higher stratas. Thus, through his encounter with the English Vegetarian Movement of the late Victorian era, which was very much a part of a wider movement involving Humanist social reforms, Gandhi not only found a rationale and ethical justification for the observance of certain Hindu dietary restrictions, but was able to relate these to a much broader context.

As Gandhi's philosophy of life matured, the vegetarianism which he advocated and practiced became more and more combined with the ethical and religious perspectives which he developed in connection with the idea of Ahimsa. The latter essentially involves a combination of non-violence, compassion, and a respect for life—both human and animal. While in Hinduism, such a concept existed only peripherally, it was the core and pivot of Jain teachings. Thus, it is hardly surprising that in his development of an Ahimsa-based philosophy and ethic, the influence of the Jain lay-philosopher, Raychandbhai Mehta, a longtime personal friend of Gandhi, was considerable. To the traditional idea of Ahimsa, Gandhi added the use of passive resistance as a means of rectifying the major evils of human society.

Even before returning to India from England, Gandhi began giving frequent public lectures, urging the adoption of a "humane diet," by which he, of course, meant a vegetarian diet. Incidently, for Gandhi as a Hindu, the latter included dairy products, but not eggs. In his lectures, he appealed to people's "best" or "highest" instincts and to basic human kindness no less than to their concerns for health and nutrition. His approach was one of gentleness, and his exhortations to at least consider adopting a non-meat diet were quite lacking in any manner of fanaticism or arrogance. What he did emphasize was that abstinence from the killing and eating of

animals was open to anyone *as a free moral choice* which was over
and above any philosophical, religious, or sectarian difference of
perspective.

As a major apostle of vegetarianism in the modern world, in
both India and the West, Gandhi can hardly be overemphasized. It
would, however, be a mistake to present him as the bearer of a
"superior Hindu ethic." As has been pointed out, his philosophy of
vegetarianism only took form in England after his contact with the
British Vegetarian Movement. The latter essentially involved a revival of the ethical vegetarian perspective advocated by some of the
most notable thinkers of Classical Greece and Rome, as combined
with newly-awakened Humanist values which sought to address
the numerous injustices and inequities of late Victorian society.
These ideals and concerns were no less alien to Hinduism than they
were to official Christianity; they were, in fact, very much at odds
with traditional Hindu values.

Gandhi's own philosophy of Ahimsa, which as we have seen,
developed out of the ancient Jain concept, somewhat surprisingly
perhaps, represented something of a new perspective for the majority of Hindus themselves; so too, did the Humanist values of the
West. What Gandhi accomplished was a fusion of both of these
within what might be termed an undefined Hindu mysticism. In
accomplishing this, Gandhi went far beyond the narrow restrictions
of caste, taboo, and mythological literalism which virtually had held
Hinduism in a moribund state for centuries.

What Gandhi did was to re-vitalize and give new form to the
best in Hinduism while rejecting and attempting to correct certain
negative phenomena. The positive, but basically un-thought-out
taboo involving the brahmanic abstention from animal flesh was
extended by Gandhi, at least ideally, to the whole of society—even
to the so-called "untouchables," whose sorrowful and unjust plight
was profoundly felt by Gandhi.

Strict adherence to a vegetarian diet was, for Gandhi, very
much a part of applying the basic principle of Ahimsa in one's daily
life. Through his efforts, millions of Hindus adopted a vegetarian
diet. While traditionally, Hindus of all castes did not eat kine, only
brahmins and religious ascetics abstained from *all* animal flesh. The
overwhelming majority of the Hindu population ate diverse animals
ranging from goats and pigs to birds and fish. Out of respect for

Gandhi and his all-inclusive application of Ahimsa to human and animal life, however, millions of middle and lower caste Hindus heeded his exhortations to adopt a strictly vegetarian diet (inclusive of dairy products, of course) and turned away from flesh-eating entirely—indeed, to such an extent that many westerners today assume that *all* Hindus are vegetarians, a state of affairs which is very far from being true.

While Gandhi is, above all, remembered for his role in the achievement of India's independence from British rule, he also stands acknowledged as a major spiritual leader and ethical giant of the still-violent 20th century. A man who himself died at the hands of an assassin, he is particularly noted for his propagation and application of his philosophy of Ahimsa in the accomplishment of Humanist political and social reforms. Indeed, he remains a major inspiration for all who seek peaceful non-violent political and social change, no less in the West than in India itself.

Gandhi differed from most western vegetarians of his time inasmuch as he always remained profoundly ascetic in his own personal orientation. Like Tolstoy, he maintained a decidedly puritanical attitude towards human sexuality and hence opposed birth control and the use of condoms. This attitude was at opposite poles from the views of such well known western vegetarians as Henry Salt, Edward Carpenter, George Bernard Shaw, and J. Howard Moore. Likewise, the quite legitimate penchant of many western vegetarians for what is sometimes described as "gourmet" vegetarian fare is not something towards which Gandhi felt any inclination. In this, he differs from most vegetarians today, the majority of whom enjoy both preparing and eating a wide variety of gourmet vegetarian dishes. In such matters, Gandhi's attitude and outlook, to a large degree, always remained that of a religious ascetic and even a "mystic," despite his intense involvement in social and political reform.

15. The Vegetarian Movement in Continental Europe

DURING THE 19TH CENTURY AND BEFORE

We have already noted in Chapters 9 and 10 that a new sensitivity to animal beings came into existence in Renaissance Italy during the 15th century. By the second half of the 16th century, in France, too, there were certain indications of a changing mentality in regard to animals. The well-known French Humanist, Michel Eyquem de Montaigne (1533-1592), for instance, encouraged a more compassionate and empathetic attitude towards the animal world in both his fables and in his essay, *On Cruelty*. He even suggests that to cause animal suffering is unethical. Although it is highly unlikely that Montaigne ever adopted a vegetarian diet, it is possible that, inasmuch as he particularly valued the wisdom of the great Plutarch, he would have supported a vegetarian movement had such a phenomenon developed in his day.

It was only during the 1700s, with the appearance of the prominent Italian physician, Antonio Cocci, a professor of medicine and philosophy in Firenze (see pages 66 and 67), that vegetarianism as such stepped boldly onto the stage of "modern" European life. His importance for the development of British vegetarianism, via the English translation of his *Dietetica Pytagorica*, has been observed in Chapter 12. In northern Europe, during the same period, the great Swedish scientist and occult philosopher, Emanuel Swedenborg (1688-1772) adopted a vegetarian diet as a personal preference. The founder of a new "school" of Christian mysticism, Swedenborg did not, however, require vegetarian observance of those who became his followers. Inasmuch as Swedenborg was not unfamiliar with the English language, it is interesting to speculate that his vegetarianism may have been inspired by the English translation of Cocci's book which he very well may have encountered during a visit to London.

In continental Europe, a vegetarian movement was slowly taking shape, although it never developed the momentum that it did in Great Britain and in North America. Quite inexplicably, the French have shown considerably less inclination towards vegetarianism than many other European peoples. Nevertheless, during the second half of the 19th century, the noted French cartographer, geographer, traveller, philosopher, and poet Elisée Reclus (1830-1905) did his best to promote a vegetarian diet in France by means of extensive public lectures, citing both ethical and nutritional reasons to abstain from animal flesh. Although Reclus did manage to convince a small number of his countrymen to follow a vegetarian diet, the fact remains that a strong vegetarian movement—such as that which came into being in Britain and the United States—never developed in France where practicing vegetarians have remained few and far between. The fact that Reclus, whose name was practically synonymous with vegetarianism, became involved in various anarchist political activities of the time may well have had a negative effect on the development of vegetarianism among the general public in France.

As for Germany, it proved to be far more fertile ground than France for vegetarianism, although less so than either Britain or North America. In 1866, the first German vegetarian society was founded by one Eduard Balzer who, like Reclus, was chiefly noted as a geographer. Balzer emphasized an ethical vegetarianism based on the "Vegetarian Fathers" of Classical Greece and Rome. No less a leading figure in the development of vegetarianism in 19th century Germany was Gustav Von Struve, author of *The Vegetable Diet* and other works promoting the vegetarian cause from an ethical point of view. Von Struve expressed no small degree of horror at the brutality involved in slaughter-house procedures as well as astonishment at the insensitivity and thoughtlessness of meat eaters who never stopped to consider that they were, in fact, devouring the corpses of once-living, feeling animal beings!

While vegetarianism came to encompass a sizable minority in Germany, and spread from there to the Netherlands, where the "Nederlandse Vegetarierbond" was founded in 1894, it made little or no headway in the Scandinavian countries until quite recently.

In Russia, the well-known novelist and non-conformist philosopher, Leo Tolstoy (1828-1910) became a champion of the vegetarian cause during the last part of his life. He also carried on a vigorous correspondence with Gandhi and spoke of his debt to the latter's philosophy of non-violence. Gandhi, on his part, acknowledged Tolstoy as a major influence on his own thought. Very much impressed by Howard William's book *The Ethics of Diet*, Tolstoy wrote a preface to the first Russian translation of it which was printed in 1892. In this, Tolstoy presents his own version of vegetarianism as set within his rather somber and puritanical philosophy of life.

There can be no doubt that Tolstoy, as a self-proclaimed "moralist," exerted a considerable influence on many, both in Russia and throughout the world, particularly in respect to his "ethics of non-violence" and his horror of war. Although Tolstoy's vegetarian concerns were, to begin with, limited to mammals or "warm-blooded quadrapeds," they gradually became more inclusive.

His Preface to William's *Ethics of Diet* includes not only a vehement condemnation of slaughter-house barbarity and a plea to the readers not to partake of this iniquity through eating the meat thus produced, but also exhortations to eschew all luxuries and "refinements," recommendations to chasten the body with fasting, and even a disparagement of enjoying one's food! Needless to say, in these matters as in his views on sexuality and indeed his revulsion towards sex, Tolstoy is quite out of line with the majority of western vegetarians of his day, particularly those of Great Britain where vegetarianism often went hand-in-hand with broader ideals of "social reform" which included "sexual liberation" and a firm stand in support of artificial birth control methods.

In any case, such divergence of views provides us with an example of the immense diversity existent among advocates of a vegetarian diet and non-violence. Whatever one may think of Tolstoy's crypto-Christian asceticism, one cannot but applaud his advocacy of non-violence, his high regard for Buddhism, his insistence upon an ethic which included treating animals with kindness and compassion (and hence not eating them), and his staunch opposition to militarism and the irrationality of war.

Indeed, there can be no doubt that Tolstoy's advocacy of vegetarianism and his campaign against the slaughterhouses had a lasting influence, if not in Russia itself, abroad where he came to have something of a "cult following" among certain persons. For him violence, militarism, war, cruelty to men and animals as well as the eating of animals are all *unnatural acts*! In this, Tolstoy, either consciously or unconsciously, looked back into the "Golden Age" of man's primordial past.

16. Vegetarianism in North America

18th–20th Century

(A) INDIGENOUS ELEMENTS

Although the author has been unable to substantiate such a theory, he intuitively senses that somewhere in North America, at least a few native Indian nations, tribes, or bands observed a strictly vegetarian diet for whatever reasons. Certain shamans also may have been vegetarian in connection with their particular status. Such persons would have been the first New World vegetarians.

While vegetarianism was gaining ground in Britain, it was also becoming known in British North America, although on a much smaller scale. Perhaps the most notable 18th century vegetarian of British North America was Timothy Ruggles (1711-1798). Born in Rochester, Massachusettes, Ruggles was a well-known Loyalist political figure and a Harvard law graduate. He was, at diverse times, a practicing attorney, an officer in the British Colonial Army who rose to the rank of general, an Associate Justice of Common Pleas, and, rather surprisingly, an innkeeper and gentleman farmer. He was also founder of an "Association of Loyal Subjects of the King"—an organization dedicated to opposing the revolutionaries and their commission of "enormous outrages upon persons and property of . . . His Majesty's peaceful subjects."[64] Persona non-grata in the breakaway Republic, where his properties had been confiscated and he himself named "a notorious conspirator" against the Republic, Ruggles fled to Nova Scotia at the age of 72 in 1784. There, at Digby, he established an enormous farm which became noteworthy for several new types of apples which he had introduced. His exceptionally good health was said to enable him to engage in work which was difficult for men half his age, even during the rugged Nova Scotia winters. As Callahan remarks: "One reason advanced for his lasting health was that he did *not eat meat* and drank no liquor, small beer excepted."[65]

Also known as a vegetarian in 18th century North America was one Joshua Evans[66] of Pennsylvania, a Quaker. Although the Society of Friends, rather surprisingly considering its philosophy of non-violence, has never required a vegetarian diet of its members, Evans' vegetarianism evidently was grounded in his Quaker mysticism. While he remained an isolated example in his times, it may be noted that today a number of Quakers observe the vegetarian way of life.

Throughout the 1800s, vegetarianism steadily gained followers in North America. There, however, it grew and developed in a notably different milleu than it did in Great Britain. In North America, for instance, a revival of interest in Classical Greco-Roman civilization—except peripherally in the field of architecture—never really caught on. Also lacking was the highly refined aesthetic sensitivity which penetrated vegetarian circles in 19th century Britain.

American vegetarianism was chiefly "practical," medical, and nutritional in nature. The majority of American vegetarians at that time simply did not connect ethics with a vegetarian diet. Nor did they see it within the context of broader Humanist concerns and "social reform." The Fabian Socialism espoused by many of those within the British vegetarian movement would have been (and no doubt was) both meaningless and puzzling to their North American counterparts. Indeed, the latter, for the most part, seemed to be hardly aware of the many social issues and needs—ranging from prison reform to remedying the various forms of injustice and exploitation suffered by factory workers and miners—which so preoccupied British vegetarians of the time along with their concern for "food reform" and the ethical treatment of animals. As for the "humane movement" itself, with its involvement in the alleviation of animal suffering (but no commitment to vegetarianism), it was perhaps even less a factor in the development of vegetarianism in North America than it was in Britain. British vegetarians included within their general "programme" of "social reform" new approaches to nearly every aspect of human life conceivable, including the active promotion of the use of prophylactics. Such a matter would have appalled the majority of American vegetarians, the latter reflecting a far more conservative, conventional point of view than their avant-garde, "liberal," and highly cultured British counterparts.

Many early North American and British vegetarians did, however, share in practicing a vegetarian diet in conjunction with a kind of "Naturism" involving "outdoor living," hiking, boating, and fresh air. Indeed, there can be no doubt that an important current within the 19th century vegetarian movement in general involved a "cult" of the strong, healthy body. From this perspective, a vegetarian diet was seen as one aspect of a broader programme involving "getting back to Nature" through camping out, regular gymnastic exercises, and cold showers.

Apparently, the first vegetarian book by a North American author was written by a certain William Metcalfe, whose *Abstinence from the Flesh of Animals* was published in 1827. Somewhat later, a prominent New England physician, Dr. William Alcott, who had been much influenced by Metcalfe, sought to enlighten the public with his own book entitled *Vegetable Diet as Sanctioned by Medical Men and Experience of All Ages*. As the title implies, Alcott's book, which was published in Boston, emphasized a vegetarian diet from a medical-nutritional perspective.

Not to be overlooked as a major figure within the early vegetarian movement of North America was Sylvester Graham (1794-1851). Graham not only promoted a vegetarian diet, but was the popularizer of unsifted whole wheat flour and bread products derived from it. He was also the inventor of the "graham cracker"— a delicious food item still available today, although its popularity has, quite inexplicably, very much declined within the last few decades. In 1850, Sylvester Graham and Dr. Alcott formed the first vegetarian society in North America. Not only were both of these gentlemen of major importance in the beginnings of the North American vegetarian movement as such, but they may also be termed the founders of the American "health food tradition."[67]

Even more important than the above individuals in regard to the popularization of vegetarian health foods were the Kellog brothers—Dr. John Harvey Kellog (1852-1943), a physician, and William K. Kellog (1860-1951), a food manufacturer and philanthropist. Both were members of the Seventh Day Adventist Church which has contributed very extensively to the growth of vegetarianism in North America both through its clear recommendation of a vegetarian diet and its endorsement and dissemination of Dr. Harvey Kellog's ideas of nutrition, health reform, and disease prevention. Not only was Dr. Kellog a tireless advocate of a meat-free diet among his patients, but he gave extensive public lectures to promote good health through following a vegetarian diet, published a magazine devoted to the same ends, and founded a health institute and sanitarium at Battle Creek, Michigan. This became a major centre for the active dissemination of knowledge pertaining to the nutritional and health aspects of vegetarianism. Major research projects pertaining to vegetarian diet, nutrition, and disease were conducted there and, in the sanitarium, diverse illnesses and diseases were healed through strict adherence to a meat-free diet. So popular did Dr. Kellog's Battle Creek centre become that he soon opened centres in other areas of the United States as well. He was particularly emphatic concerning the high nutritional value of soy beans as well as different kinds of nuts.

Together with his brother, William K. Kellog, the food manufacturer, he invented and produced a number of vegetarian "health foods." The first of these was peanut butter which was to become an extremely popular food among the entire population of North America. Its importance for vegetarians lies in its exceptionally high protein content. Although the Kellog brothers were the first to make peanut butter avilable as a manufactured or processed commodity in the modern world, peanuts ground into a paste were first used among the ancient Incas.

The second type of "health food" invented, produced, and popularized to some small degree by the Kellog brothers and their researchers consisted of various types of canned processed soy bean products. Considerably different from the presently very popular oriental soy bean product, tofu or bean curd—which had been produced by the Chinese and Japanese in North America for some time, chiefly for their own use—the Kellog soy products were no less nutritious and pleasing to the palate than their oriental counterparts. Inasmuch as tofu and tempeh have only become widely available to the American public during the last three decades, the first soy bean products to which American vegetarians were exposed were produced by the Kellogs. Some of these canned items are still available today under the "Loma Linda" label. To a large extent, however, they remained too expensive to become a really popular food. Even today, they cost, quite inexplicably, twice as much or more than packaged fresh oriental bean curd or tempeh. Nevertheless, the Kellog soybean products can be viewed as an important step forward in the creation of a high-protein "meat substitute."

Although the Kellog brothers vegetarianism was overwhelmingly medical-nutritional in nature, ethical considerations and concern for the animal world have gradually become greater over the years among the Seventh Day Adventists, and today are by no means lacking. Not without significance in this respect is the fact that William Kellog set up and endowed a major bird sanctuary in Michigan.

It may be observed that today, the Seventh Day Adventists represent the largest Christian denomination which advocates (although does not require) a strictly vegetarian diet. It is to be hoped that in the near future, other Christian churches may adopt such an enlightened attitude.

Notably different from the vegetarianism of the Kellog brothers and the Seventh Day Adventist Church was the Humanist vegetarianism of J. Howard Moore (1862-1916) whose book *The Unusual Kinship* was published in 1908 by Charles Kerr and Co. of Chicago. A zoologist and fervent Darwinian, Moore was a philosopher and popularizer of evolution and the essential unity of earthly life-forms, emphasizing the vestigial similarities and the recapitulations of simpler life forms in human development. From such phenomena, he derived his views concerning man's kinship with all animal beings. An American, J. Howard Moore was a friend of the British Humanist, Henry Salt. Both espoused basically the same values, including a strong sense of moral obligation towards the animal world and, by extension, the ethical necessity of maintaining a vegetarian diet. Like Salt, Moore emphasized man's need to live in harmony with Nature and found himself in total disagreement with the traditional Christian perspective and what he saw as its decidedly lacking sense of ethic. Moore's influence was perhaps greatest in the academic world as well as in certain avant-garde "bohemian" circles involved in theatre and the arts.

Moore illustrates the extent to which Darwinian theory can be utilized in promoting the vegetarian cause. Darwin, he states, has established the unity and "common sanguinity of life." Thus, man's Humanist ideals must be extended to the entire animal world on the grounds of "universal kinship." "Earth-life," he observes, "is a single process" and "the earth belongs . . . to the beings who inhabit it—*to all of them.*"[68]

Moore decries as monstrous the frequently encountered view of animals as "commodities" to be used and exploited. They are, he states, "looked upon as mere things . . . they may be set upon, beaten, maimed, starved, assassinated, eaten, deceived, imprisoned, robbed, tormented, skinned alive, shot down for a pastime, cut to pieces out of curiousity, or compelled to undergo any other enormity or victimization man can think of."[69] At man's "cannibalistic feasts," he observes, the reprobate even "discuss the flavour of animals!"[70]

Mentioning the Compassion of the Buddha, Moore notes that "the doctrine of universal kinship is not a new doctrine. It is as old as human philosophy. It was taught by the Buddha twenty-four hundred years ago . . . and it was taught by Pythagoras." "Civilized" human beings, he advises, should rise above the barbaric and primitive activities of war, fighting, hunting, fishing, torturing, and killing. No civilized man or woman should "be indifferent to the sufferings of others or find delight in such loathsome avocations as the fishing or hunting of their fellow creatures."[71]

Moore was concerned that man overcome the brutal and barbaric sadism of the hunt. "No human being," he writes, should enjoy seeing a pack of hounds hunt down and rend to pieces a poor harmless hare—unless he were a savage. No human being should go out to the abodes of the squirrel or quail and shoot murderous balls into their bodies . . . unless he were a savage. No human being would lounge all day about the margin of a brook . . . in order to thrust brutal hooks into the lips of those whom he deceives and drag them from the waters to suffocate in the sun—unless he were a savage."[72]

Before turning to the influences from the East which contributed to the development of the vegetarian movement in the United States during the late 19th and early 20th centuries, something should be said concerning vegetarianism in Canada where, it would seem that a vegetarian movement, as such, was much later in taking root than in Great Britain and the United States. Nevertheless, as has been noted in the second paragraph of Chapter 16, even as early as the late 18th century, vegetarianism was not unknown in that area of North America which was to become Canada, thanks to such distinguished vegetarians as Timothy Ruggles (1711-1798). A well-known Massachusettes Loyalist and Harvard graduate who immigrated to Nova Scotia after the American Revolution, Ruggles might well be viewed as a kind of "patron founder" of vegetarianism in Canada.

Although there would seem to be no evidence concerning the existence of Canadian vegetarians during the 1800s, this certainly does not mean that there were none, but only that they remained very "low key," as it were. The reason for this perhaps lies in the fact that Canadians tend to be both more private and more "individualistic" than either the British or Americans. Thus, to begin with, Canadian vegetarians seem to have been considerably less inclined to organize themselves in groups or associations than were vegetarians residing in Britain or the United States. Consequently, it was only in the year 1911 that a Canadian organization dedicated to the vegetarian cause came into existence. This occurred in the city of Toronto, Ontario. The name of the organization was "The Food Reform League," the name perhaps being indicative of the British mentality which saw vegetarianism as one specific need within a much wider programme of Humanist social reform. Unfortunately, this organization went out of existence during World War I.

Quietly and unobtrusively, however, individual vegetarians continued to carry on the vegetarian way of life on a non-organized basis until the 40s and 50s of this century when vegetarian associations began appearing throughout Canada, the first, once again, coming into existence in Toronto. For information on vegetarianism in contemporary Canada, the reader is referred to Chapter 17, p. 119.

(B) INFLUENCES FROM THE EAST

Along with the diverse indigenous influences which entered into the formation of the American vegetarian movement were various currents from India and the East, often as filtered through and re-structured by the western mind. Chief among these at the end of the last century and for the first decades of the present one was the Theosophical Society which had been founded by the Russian eccentric, Madame Blavatsky in the 1880s. Her successor as head of the Society was Annie Besant (1847-1933), who was a leading figure in the British Vegetarian Society. It was she who extensively propagated the Theosophical Movement in the United States, where it came to flourish to a far greater degree than it did in the British Isles. Indeed, around the turn of the century and well into the first three decades of this century, it offered what was to many, an attractive alternative to the major Christian denominations as a possible "spiritual path." What concerns us here is the fact that, while not requiring vegetarianism of its members, it nevertheless, particularly under the guidance of Annie Besant, encouraged and endorsed the adoption of a vegetarian diet.

The Theosophical Movement essentially involved a synthetic religious perspective of a very syncretistic nature. In it, certain basic elements of Hinduism and Buddhism were incorporated with diverse aspects of "spiritualism" and the occult world of psychical research as well as many ideas deriving from western Humanism and Darwin's theory and philosophy of evolution. In North America, during the 50 years between the 1880s and the 1930s, the Theosophical Society became fairly large. Its membership consisted chiefly of a more or less conservative, affluent, and moderately well-educated element of American society. Although men were by no means lacking in it, women predominated. The wives of industrialists, business magnates, and university professors figured prominently in the Society as did various individuals with specific interests in India and the Orient as well as persons with a penchant for psychical research and the occult. Many, but by no means all, members of the Society were dedicated vegetarians.

After the 1920s, membership in the Theosophical Society steadily dwindled as did the vegetarian movement itself in North America. Only during the 1960s did vegetarianism on that continent begin to undergo a revival. During the 40-year interim, various elements kept vegetarianism alive there. These included both the Seventh Day Adventists and members of various Hindu-oriented sects. The importance of the Seventh-Day Adventists in this respect cannot be overestimated, particularly inasmuch as their membership continued to grow during that period—and with it, the observance of a vegetarian diet, which they did not actually require of their members, but certainly very much encouraged. Indeed, many of the few-and-far-between vegetarian health food stores of that period were run by them.

Among the vegetarian-oriented spiritual organizations from India which stepped forward to take the place of Theosophy in North America was the Vedanta Society. This highly metaphysical and profoundly philosophical organization had already established itself in the United States not long after the turn of the century, and continued to grow for some time. Although relatively small in number, the Vedantists served as a reminder, to all who encountered them, that vegetarianism was a viable alternative to a carnivorous diet.

With the coming of the so-called "Counterculture" of the 60s, a number of small Hindu-oriented groups and movements, headed by various swamis and "spiritual masters," came to enjoy a certain popularity throughout North America. Most of these advocated a vegetarian diet either as a required practice or at least as a preferable ideal. Chief among such religious groups was the "Krishna Consciousness Movement," the importance of which for vegetarianism in general is undeniable. Not only does this spiritual organization require a vegetarian diet of its followers, but it has popularized vegetarian cuisine through dispensing free vegetarian meals to the public at its ashrams and at public festivals. Its adherents have also produced a number of excellent vegetarian cookbooks.

Not to be overlooked among the diverse religious groups of Indian origin, which have helped to spread the vegetarian way of life in North America, is the Kirpal Light Satsang organization. Many persons dedicated to realizing in their lives the teachings of its founder, Sant Thakar Singh, are to be found in both Canada and the United States. Vegetarianism is very much a part of their lifestyle, and in many places, members of this movement have run organic food stores as well as quality vegetarian restaurants. By means of such outlets, a wide range of vegetarian foods from around the world have been introduced and made known in North America.

As for the so-called "Macrobiotic Movement" of George Oshawa, although many of its followers are vegetarians, they are not obliged to be entirely so. The fact is that the "Macrobiotic Movement" cannot in itself be termed strictly vegetarian. Despite its laudable emphasis on grains and green vegetables as well as on various high protein soybean products such as tofu and tempeh, the "Macrobiotic Diet" allows fish and even more astonishingly, "wild birds" while banning eggplant, tomatoes, and nutritious milk products. Thus, in allowing the consumption of our avian and picean brethren, Oshawa has distanced his philosophy of diet from genuine vegetarianism and the ethical considerations upon which it is based. Nevertheless, all vegetarians may be grateful to Oshawa and his followers for popularizing not only tempeh, tofu, and diverse grains—which have become major vegetarian staples—but also arame and other Japanese sea vegetables.

(C) THE JEWISH CONTRIBUTION

Inasmuch as Jewish vegetarianism is primarily, although by no means exclusively, a modern North American phenomenon, there being a far greater number of Jewish vegetarians in North America than elsewhere, it would seem appropriate to include this section within the chapter on the development of vegetarianism in North America.

To some, the existence of a Jewish vegetarian movement may come as something of a surprise. Indeed, one might expect that an ethically-based vegetarianism would be as rare among Jews as it is among Christians. Such, however, is not the case. Actually, an inclination towards vegetarianism is far more frequent among Jews, both "observant" and "non-observant," than it is among Christians, particularly those of the more traditional mainline denominations. The observance of a vegetarian diet is also something more accepted as a way of life on the part of the non-vegetarian majority of Jews than it is among their Christian counterparts.

As Jonathan Wolf, a leader of the North American Jewish Vegetarian Society, points out in an interview with the *New York Times* (see *N.Y. Times*, June 14/1977, Living Section—"When Keeping Kosher Isn't Kosher Enough"), *no less than two Chief Rabbis of Israel have been vegetarians!* This fact in itself should speak eloquently in behalf of the legitimacy of observing a strictly vegetarian diet within a traditional Orthodox Jewish millieu! After all, no where in the Old Testament or the Talmud are Jews *commanded* to eat meat. Notwithstanding this fact, many devout Jews tend to remain very "low key" concerning their vegetarianism so as not to create a gulf between themselves and those who do not follow such a diet.

A vegetarian element has been present in Judaism from very ancient times. At least a few of those adhering to the Essene Sect, which was very much opposed to animal sacrifice in the Temple, are said to have observed a strictly vegetarian diet, although some claim that this is entirely a matter of conjecture. More to the point is the fact that during the 19th century, various Hassidic spiritual leaders and their followers in Poland made vegetarianism a part of their way of life, for reasons of both ethics and health. We have already mentioned Lewis Gompertz, the philanthropist and leader of the Humane Movement, as a leading and very dedicated Jewish vegetarian in England during the first half of the 19th century. Very different from Gompertz, but no less an adherent of vegetarianism was the Warsaw intellectual and writer, Melech Ravich, who was the editor of a Yiddish literary review, "Literarishe Bletter" during the 1920s. Ravich was a Humanist and vegetarian activist who looked towards a future society wherein a united mankind dedicated to the weal of all—Jews and non-Jews, men and animals— would prevail over the violence, disharmony, and inequities so prevalent in the society of his day. With the immigration of many Jewish people to New York from Poland around the turn of the century, at least a few of whom were vegetarians of an either Hassidic or secular Humanist outlook, the stage was set for the development of a Jewish vegetarianism in North America. Indeed, the 20th century witnessed a remarkable increase in vegetarian sentiment and observance among North American (and to a lesser degree, European) Jews, both Reformed and Orthodox, Hassidic and non-Hassidic, observant and non-observant. Today, there are many thousands of Jewish vegetarians, some religious and some non-religious, in North America alone. Thus, the Jewish contribution to contemporary vegetarianism can scarcely be overlooked.

A number of internationally-known Jewish intellectuals, scientists, musicians, literary figures, and philosophers who strictly observed a vegetarian diet helped give a certain impetus to the Jewish vegetarian movement in North America and elsewhere, despite the fact that most remained notably "low key" concerning their vegetarianism. These included scientist and philosopher Albert Einstein (1879-1952), writer Isaac Bashevis Singer, violinist Yehudi Menuin, and Martin Buber (1878-1965) who was a philosopher and transmitter of Hassidic tales.

Here, it may be observed that the maintenence of a vegetarian diet is, unquestionably, far more difficult for the "observant" Jew than for the non-Jewish vegetarian, inasmuch as the basic vegetarian diet must be kept within the framework of certain Kosher rules and customs. Various vegetarian staples, for instance, ranging from leavened bread to lentils, corn, millet, and rice cannot be eaten during the observance of Passover according to Askenazic rules.

Beginning with the 40s and 50s of this century, numerous Jewish vegetarian-restaurants came into being in the eastern part of the United States. Later, such establishments spread to other areas of North America which have large Jewish populations as well as to

Israel and to the major urban centres of Britain and continental Europe. While many Jewish vegetarians joined non-sectarian vegetarian societies or associations, others have chosen to form specifically Jewish vegetarian societies. These are particularly evident in the eastern US and Canada. Among these is the North American Jewish Vegetarian Society, which is affiliated with the London-centred Jewish Vegetarian Society which has members worldwide.

The renowned novelist and short story writer, Isaac Bashevis Singer (1904-1991) provides us with an outstanding example of modern Jewish vegetarianism in the midst of American life. Due to the voluminous quantity of fictional and autobiographical writing which he produced, the foundations of his vegetarianism are not difficult to ascertain. Singer often reveals himself and his philosophy of life within the framework of his stories and the diversity of characters and situations that they contain. In Singer's *Enemies, A Love Story*,[73] the sentiments expressed by one of the main characters, Herman, are undoubtedly his own. In one section of this story, Herman watches the fishermen return with the prey they had taken—pitiful creatures who not long before had been enjoying life in the depths of the sea. Now, they were but bloodied corpses on the decks of the boats, their eyes glazed and bloated in the sun. The killers of these lifeless beings stood about weighing their victims. Herman noted to himself that most men, in their dealings with other species, were Nazis, their actions manifesting an undisguised racism and wholly unacceptable barbarism. Herman vowed that he would henceforth be a vegetarian.

This brings up an interesting phenomenon—namely, that the dreadful Holocaust experienced by the Jews of Europe, to some degree, brought about an increase in vegetarianism within the Jewish community. Certain survivors of the death camps are said to have turned to a vegetarian diet out of empathy with the innocent beasts transported to the tortures of the slaughterhouse via the same cattle cars on which they themselves were brought to the Nazi death camps.

Although first exposed to vegetarianism in the midst of Jewish life in Poland, both among the Hassidim and among secular Humanists such as the previously-mentioned Melech Ravich with whom he lodged in Warsaw, Singer only adopted the vegetarian way of life himself after emigrating to America and taking up residence in New York.

He felt that either the commandment, "Thou shalt not kill" should be extended to include all animals, or that a new commandment should be introduced—namely, one which specifically forbids the harming, killing, eating, and exploitation of animals. He notes, with astonishment, that man could even think of mercy, beg for mercy in his prayers, and pretend to Humanist values and concerns when he sheds the blood of innocent animals and eats their pitiful corpses.[74]

Often, in his stories, Singer extols the "patience" and the awesome "innocence" of animals. He was especially fond of birds, and in his story *The Letter Writer*, old Herman—who lies ill with pneumonia and whose sentiments are those of Singer himself had he been in such a situation—worries that the little mouse, for which he was in the habit of putting out bits of cheese end cracker, might starve. The smallest act of kindness and compassion directed towards the least of animal beings, he saw as no less significant than a major act of beneficence towards a human being. Singer came to believe that anyone who was sufficiently insensitive to kill a chicken or a lamb might also not be above killing a man.[75]

He felt animal and human suffering very keenly, looking out as he did from the emotional, near-legendary world of Eastern European Jewry with its constant interplay of light and darkness, its perpetual sense of impending catastrophe, its bloody world of ritual animal slaughter (so very abhorrent and perplexing to Jewish vegetarians), the rapid passionate music and dances of its wedding celebrations, and the ecstatic mystical transport of its Hassidic rabbis. As Kresh observes, there is within the intensity and archetypal quality of Eastern European Jewish life, a chemerical "trompe d'oeil" quality. What is more, one might suggest that within the latter, there was also present a sense of "Divine caprice" which might anytime loose itself in the midst of that life, bringing either ecstasy or horror. It was out of such a world that Isaac Bashevis Singer and his vegetarian way of life eventually emerged.

His ethically-based vegetarianism had more in common with that which prevailed among British and continental vegetarians at the end of the last century than it did with the health and nutrition oriented vegetarianism which prevailed among the majority of American vegetarians until relatively recently. So too, the asceticism of Gandhi and Tolstoy was something quite alien to Singer, for whom both sexuality and eating were activities which are meant to be enjoyed. The important thing for Isaac Bashevis Singer was not to harm one's fellow beings, whether animals or humans, and at the same time to enjoy life to the full, rejoicing in its harmless pleasures. He appreciated not only fine vegetarian cuisine, but also an occasional glass or two of wine.

17. Vegetarianism in the Contemporary World— Capsule Summaries*

WESTERN EUROPE

The oldest vegetarian movements in continental Europe are those of Germany and the Netherlands. Today, the largest number of vegetarians in Western Europe are within those two countries, both of which have active vegetarian organizations, extensive publications, and numerous vegetarian food outlets and restaurants in major urban centres as well as smaller towns. In both places, many diverse vegetarian perspectives are represented, including that of a Christian vegetarian denomination founded by the Danish Lutheran pastor, Carl Anders Skriver. This group, known as the Nazoreans, is dedicated to the principle of non-violence and the consequent observance of a strictly vegetarian diet as well as a simplicity of lifestyle.

Unquestionably, one of the most prominent German vegetarians of this century was the altruistic medical doctor and baroque musicologist, Albert Schweitzer (1875-1965), who spent the major portion of his life in equitorial Africa alleviating sickness and disease gratis among the native population. Schweitzer elaborated his own philosophy of "reverence for life," adapting the eastern idea of Ahimsa to his own personal interpretation of Christianity. His distinctly ethical vegetarianism emerged as one aspect of this adaptation.

In Scandinavia, as well as in Belgium, the situation is very different from that in Germany and the Netherlands. In the former areas, what interest in vegetarianism exists, is relatively recent, and the number of vegetarians extremely small. There are said to be more vegetarians in Sweden and Denmark than elsewhere

* The information given in this chapter is derived chiefly, but not exclusively, from newsletters of the Vegetarian Union of North America and the International Vegetarian Union.

in Scandinavia, with a growing vegetarian society in Stockholm. However, a few individuals who observe a vegetarian diet can be found throughout the Scandinavian countries. There are even occasional vegetarian restaurants. The author can remember an excellent establishment of this nature in Rekjavik, Iceland, which was patronized by foreign vegetarian tourists as well as by native Icelandic vegetarians.

Although the various Scandinavian peoples are not large consumers of mammal flesh, fish has always played a major part in their diets and cuisines. Their fondness for fish as well as the fact that the fishing industry is of major importance in their economies seems to make any great extension of vegetarianism in these lands problematic to say the least. Much the same may be said of modern Greece and Portugal—also lands where fish is a dietary staple and fishing of immense importance to the respective economies.

The future of vegetarianism in all these lands would seem to depend upon the development of some manner of "sea-flavoured," "fish-textured" vegetarian substitute (perhaps containing various types of seaweed as a major ingredient) as well as coming up with new major industries which could replace the fishing industry in these country's economies. There is ample room here for the creative endeavours of persons capable of new ideas and inventive fresh approaches to the problem.

As for France, despite the extensive work around the turn of the century on the part of the great French apostle of vegetarianism, Elisee Reclus, it would seem that vegetarianism has never really caught on there. As elsewhere, individual vegetarians undoubtedly exist, but any extensive network of vegetarian activists or organization of vegetarian groups would seem to be quite lacking. Nor are many specifically vegetarian food shops to be found. The author has heard that in all of Paris, there is only one exclusively vegetarian restaurant!

There is, however, a major vegetarian centre with library, accomodations, and excellent vegetarian fare in Normandy, near La Havre. The name of this centre is "Le Moulon Foulon." Interestingly enough, a Vegetarian Association, consisting of some 60 people, has recently come into existence in the city of Nice in southeast France. The founder is a Swedish resident of that city, Arne Wingquist. It is his intention to organize vegetarian associations in other French urban centres as well.

In Spain, a land without any vegetarian antecedents, there is an increased interest in vegetarianism, although as yet, actual vegetarians are few. Most of those who observe a vegetarian diet in Spain are members of an organization dedicated to the esoteric teachings of Pythagoras—namely, the "Gran Fraternidad Universal"* which is chiefly active in South America. This group promotes the universal practice of vegetarianism within the context of Pythagorean ethics and philosophy. It was founded by the French physician, Dr. Serge Reynauld de la Ferrier, whose movement has elicited considerable interest in South America, some in Spain, and none whatever in his native France.

In Italy, which has very ancient vegetarian antecedents in the Pythagorean communities of Cretona and elsewhere in southern Italy when this area was part of "Greater Greece," the vegetarian movement today is said to be gaining momentum. It is inspired by the great genius, Leonardo Da Vinci, by the father of western vegetarianism, Pythagoras himself, and by the 18th century Italian physician, Antonio Cocci, whose book *Dietetica Pytagorica* or *The Pythagorean Diet* was published in Firenze in 1743, with an English edition coming out in London in 1745, as has been noted in Chapter 12. This volume helped prepare the way for the British Vegetarian Movement of the 19th century.

Today, the "Associazione Vegetarina Italiana" actively seeks to promote the vegetarian way of life in Italy. It is worth observing here that considering the fact that the Italian cuisine so splendidly lends itself to an enormous variety of delectable vegetarian dishes, one can only express astonishment that a full-fledged vegetarian movement did not long ago sweep over the entire Italian peninsula.

INDIA

Although certain segments of the Indian population—notably religious ascetics, the brahmin caste, all members of the Jain Religion and certain Hindu sects and sub-sects—have observed a vegetarian diet over the centuries, the majority of the Hindu population was by no means vegetarian, although they did not kill or eat kine. Thanks to Gandhi's widespread programme of enlightenment in-

---

* See p. 109 of the Latin American section of the present chapter for more on this organization and its founder.

volving the propagation of the principle of Ahimsa throughout all segments of the Hindu population, however, perhaps a bare majority of Hindus today observe a strictly vegetarian diet, inclusive, of course, of dairy products.

Vegetarianism is, in fact, today a way of life so common in India that it is completely accepted by Indian society at large without predjudice or detrimental attitudes which are so common on the part of non-vegetarians in the West. Many hotels and restaurants throughout India even maintain separate vegetarian kitchens.

There is, of course, no problem whatever in obtaining vegetarian foods throughout India. Indian cuisine, in general, is in fact to a very large degree vegetarian. Here one may observe that the extension of this vegetarian cuisine to both the UK and North America has proved to be of tremendous benefit to western vegetarians. So too, the spread of various Hindu-oriented religious organizations which emphasize the observance of a vegetarian diet have done much to further vegetarianism in general throughout the western world, but particularly in North America and Great Britain.

India is certainly an important centre of vegetarianism in the world today. Even entirely vegetarian villages are not unknown. One such village, Chanda Prabhu, for instance, exists near Madras. Yet, to a considerable degree, vegetarianism in India today is something simply taken for granted. Organized vegetarian groups dedicated to actively promoting vegetarian enlightenment, although existent in some areas, are not particularly popular. Unfortunately, the Indian Government does not share the vegetarian sentiments of the majority of its population and—*like governments everywhere*—attempts to promote a non-vegetarian diet, particularly encouraging the rearing and eating of birds!

The Manker International Foundation does, however, carry on an extensive programme in both India and throughout the world to promote the vegetarian way of life in memory of Sri J. N. Manker or "Mankerji" who died in 1972. He was a major figure in the promotion of vegetarian ethic. Today, perhaps the leading vegetarian activist in India is the renowned Sri Surendra Mehta.

While the overwhelming majority of observant vegetarians in India are either Jains or Hindus, it is worth noting that least a few

Sikhs* and Ismailis+—neither of whom are required by the rules of their respective religions to be vegetarian—nevertheless observe a vegetarian diet out of personal preference. Vegetarianism, it may be observed, is either lacking entirely or is all but non-existent among adherents of the usual forms of Islamic orthodoxy throughout the Islamic world. A small vegetarian society, does, however, exist in Tehran. It was founded in 1963 by Mr. J. Ermian Kharaabati who died this year (1993) and who wrote many books and articles on the subject.

SRI LANKA

In Sri Lanka, the Sri Kapila Humanitarian Society carries on a major vegetarian enlightenment program among the general public, emphasizing the advantages of a vegetarian diet from both medical and ethical perspectives. The Society is headed by a Mr. G. A. de Silva and it has over 5,000 members. No less important than its vegetarian awareness programs is its opposition to all forms of cruelty towards animals.

AFRICA

While adherence to a vegetarian diet is an unknown phenom-enon in *most* of Africa, even there, a few vegetarians exist. Despite the fact that for the overwhelming majority of the population, the whole concept of vegetarianism as a way of life as well as any sense of man's ethical obligation to the animal world are quite non-existent, a few small vegetarian societies have emerged, often under the guidance of persons from India. These vegetarian associations are in Nigeria, Lagos, and Tanzania. The most recent is one which was formed in Nairobi, Kenya by East Indian residents, with the assistance of the "Young Indian Vegetarians of Britain Association."

To a large degree, it would seem that what little vegetarianism does exist in Africa is, in fact, very closely associated with local East Indian communities, many members of which are followers of Gandhi's principle of Ahimsa or Non-Violence in all spheres of life. This undoubtedly is indicative of the special "mission" of persons

---

* Members of a monotheistic faith founded in the 16th century by Guru Nanak.

+ An esoteric religious group which exists on the farthest periphery of the Islamic world and is headed by the Aga Khan.

from India in bringing vegetarianism and the vegetarian ethic to the enormous native population of Africa. Recently, one may note, a vegetarian society has also come into existence in nearby Mauritius.

LATIN AMERICA

Even in Latin America, a vegetarian movement exists, and there is evidence of a growing interest. In Panama, vegetarianism is said to be particularly strong. Other vegetarian centres in Latin America include Venezuela, Chile, and Columbia. Individual vegetarians as well as small vegetarian groups are, of course, present throughout Latin America as they are throughout most of the world. It is only in the above Latin American countries, however, that active vegetarian movements are sufficiently strong to successfully leave an imprint on the societies in which they exist.

Both Caracus and the mountain city of Merida in Venezuela are major areas of vegetarian activism. Many excellent vegetarian restaurants are said to exist in both cities. In Venezuela, vegetarianism is closely involved with a strong environmental and ecological awareness, particularly in regard to the preservation of the rainforests and the protection of the latter from the depredations inflicted on them by the enormously powerful cattle ranchers. Indeed, it is not without danger to be an environmentalist vegetarian activist there. According to the newsletter of the International Vegetarian Union of August/91, lives are sometimes forfeited for involvement in such activities.

Both in Venezuela and elsewhere throughout Latin America, particularly in Chile, many vegetarians are members of a group calling itself the "Naturistas," who combine a strictly vegetarian diet with "natural hygene" and living "close to Nature." Many Naturistas, for instance, promote the practice of nudism when circumstances permit. Although the Venezuelan Naturistas eat only uncooked fruits and vegetables, those in Chile eat cooked vegetarian foods as well. Naturistas also exist in Bolivia, but it is Bogota, Columbia which is seen by many as the "vegetarian capital" of South America, with a larger number of vegetarian food outlets than elsewhere. Local vegetarian specialities include various types of vegetable tamales. Several excellent vegetarian restaurants also may be found in Santiago, Chile.

No less significant than the Naturistas in contributing to the development of vegetarianism throughout Latin America is the already mentioned organization termed the "Gran Fraternidad Universal," founded by the prominent French doctor and scientist, Serge Reynauld de la Ferrier. This society is dedicated to promoting the spiritual transformation of the individual and the world through reviving the ancient esoteric wisdom of Pythagoras. The adoption and promotion of a strictly vegetarian diet is viewed as of primary importance in the desired transformation of human life and society. Thus, members of the Gran Fraternidad Universal operate vegetarian food outlets and restaurants in many areas of South America. They also conduct vegetarian cooking classes. Over and above all this, the fraternity serves as a Pythagorean initiatory organization.

EASTERN EUROPE

A new day has finally dawned for vegetarianism in Eastern Europe, and once again, the path of Non-Violence and vegetarianism fostered by Leo Tolstoy at the end of the last century and the beginning of this one can resume its natural course of development—rather curiously, long after vegetarianism has been abandoned as an integral part of Tolstoyan ideology by many who consider themselves followers of Tolstoy in the United States.

Estonia, on the shores of the Baltic, is proving to be an especially fertile ground for the propagation and practice of the vegetarian way of life. The city of Tallinn is the centre of vegetarian activities there, the local vegetarian organization being composed chiefly, although not exclusively, of persons whose orientation is essentially Tolstoyan—persons for whom opposition to all forms of war and violence go hand in hand with the observance of a vegetarian diet. Headed by Kristina Luite, the Tallinn Vegetarian Society runs a vegetarian cafeteria and maintains on the same premises a vegetarian food shop where organically-grown vegetables are available when in season. The name of the entire enterprise is "Vegetaris."

A small vegetarian movement exists in Latvia, while in Lithuania, an important centre of vegetarian enlightenment has come into being in the city of Palanga. It assumes the form of a health resort which promotes the restoration of man's sense of harmony with the universe as well as his natural health through the observance of a strictly vegetarian diet combined with extensive walking or jogging in the nearby pine forests. The director is a Mr. Dainius Kepanis.

In Russia proper, there is a growing interest in and practice of vegetarianism. Consequently, a powerful vegetarian movement has taken shape in various areas, but particularly in Moscow itself. The All-Union Vegetarian Society in Russia, sometimes termed simply The Vegetarian Society in Russia, held its founding congress in December/1990, thanks to the policies of liberalization put into effect by Gorbachev, even being granted official status as a recognized organization due to its ecological concerns which form a major aspect of its particular vegetarian approach. Since the demise of the Soviet Union, it has continued to thrive and grow. The present president of the society is Tatyana Pavlova, and among the society's activities can be mentioned the publication of numerous books on vegetarianism, nutrition, and meatless cuisine. The society is also extensively involved in both creating alternatives to the use of animals in laboratory research and in operating a medical centre which is engaged in preventative and diagnostic medicine from a strictly vegetarian perspective. Active branches of the society also exist in St. Petersburg and Nijni-Novgorod as well as in the Altai and western Siberia.

Although the membership of the Vegetarian Society in Russia includes persons of many different philosophical perspectives, more than a few of the members are oriented towards the teachings of Leo Tolstoy. Indeed, Anatoly Gorelov, who is President of the Moscow Tolstoy Society (a quite separate organization) is a leading figure among the Moscow vegetarians. He hopes to eventually see a major vegetarian centre with a library, regular lectures, and a vegetarian restaurant established there in connection with the Moscow Tolstoy Society.

It may be noted here that for the entirety of its existence, the Soviet State, like all other Communist regimes—and, incidentally, the Governments of the USA and the UK as well—actively promoted meat-eating and the "cattle industry," thus flying in the face of not only Humanist ethic, but of ecological reality and good health as well.

In Poland, where vegetarianism remained weak and undeveloped for many years, there is currently considerable interest in it. The Honourable Maxwell Lee of the International Vegetarian

Union, during a lecture tour of Poland in Spring/93, reports rapidly growing vegetarian societies in many Polish towns and cities, with his lecture tours, in some cases attracting over 300 persons. He notes that there are two excellent vegetarian restaurants in Warsaw, and one in Krakow.

Even Bulgaria and Romania have a few vegetarians, although as an activist movement, vegetarianism remains extremely weak in both places. In Hungary, it is somewhat stronger, with a Vegetarian Society in Budapest. By-in-large Poland, Romania, and Hungary all remain extremely heavy consumers of meat. Yet, given the right leadership and a hoped-for coming into existence of dynamic vegetarian activists, all these lands may eventually develop strong vegetarian organizations.

Somewhat surprisingly, it is to Czechoslovakia, a land whose cuisine leans heavily towards meat dishes, that we must look for the largest and best organized vegetarian movement in Eastern Europe. This is particularly true of the Slovaks, some 4,000 of whom not only observe a vegetarian diet, but are members of an extremely activist vegetarian organization, the headquarters of which are in Bratislava, the capitol of Slovakia. A prominent medical doctor, Igor Bukovsky of Bratislava heads the organization which prints a monthly magazine, popularizes the health and nutritional aspect of the vegetarian diet by means of extensive public lectures, and is attempting to introduce various soy bean products to the general population in shops and at food fairs, urging people to try them as meat substitutes. The response has been most enthusiastic and Slovak vegetarians are currently attempting to attract investment from abroad in vegetarian food products. As it is, the demand far exceeds the supply, with long queues at vegetarian food shops.

Close ties are maintained between the Slovak Vegetarian Association and the much smaller, yet still substantial, Vegetarian Society of the Czechs which is located in Prague. Dr. Peter Pribis, who has long sought to show that meat consumption is a leading cause of disease, is the leading vegetarian activist there.

THE CHINESE

This section on Chinese vegetarianism in the contemporary world is different from the other sections in this chapter inasmuch as it is not limited to a specific geographic location, but rather encompasses the Chinese as a people wherever they are. Thus, it not only deals with China itself, but also with Taiwan, Hong Kong, Singapore, and numerous Chinese enclaves or communities in North America and throughout the world.

To begin with, it may be observed that Chinese vegetarianism is virtually synonymous with Chinese Buddhism, being intimately bound up with Chinese Buddhist observance. In other words, the two go hand in hand. Wherever there are Chinese, inevitably *at least a few will be practicing Buddhists and, consequently, observant vegetarians.* Indeed, despite its minority status, Chinese Buddhism even today remains very much a living religion for many thousands of Chinese, both in China and beyond its borders. What is more, Buddhism has left a powerful imprint on Chinese life and civilization. Nor, due to the Chinese penchant for religious syncretism, is it unusual for non-Buddhists to include images of Gautama Buddha and the Bodhisattva Kwan-Yin in family shrines or on popular Taoist altars. Nearly all Chinese even today, except those who profess to be either Christian or anti-religious, possess a certain reverence for Kwan-Yin, the Bodhisattva of Compassion, who is seen by Buddhists as the special patron of animals and of vegetarianism itself. One wonders if perhaps this indicates, on some level, the acceptance of vegetarianism *as an ideal,* even if an ideal only attainable among the observant Buddhist minority.

Traditionally Chinese Buddhists have, over the centuries, been the strictest vegetarians of the Buddhist world. Although strict vegetarian observance is said to no longer prevail among *all* Buddhists in mainland China as an ethical absolute, there can be no question that it continues to be observed by both Buddhist monks and the majority of devout lay people. In Taiwan, Hong Kong, Singapore, and in the numerous Chinese communities of North America, for a practicing Chinese Buddhist to be anything but a strict vegetarian would be quite unthinkable!

Even in China proper, vegetarianism remains the rule rather than the exception among Buddhists. Wang Chang Qing, a resident of Shanghai and a prominent member of the I.V.U. or International Vegetarian Union, notes in several newsletters of that organization, the continuing existence of Buddhist vegetarian restaurants in China, specifically citing one in Hangzhou as well as several in the city of Shanghai which are operated by major Buddhist temples.

Such restaurants continue to provide vegetarian fare in many Chinese urban centres and even in outlying country areas in connection with Buddhist shrines and monasteries.

Recently, in May/93, during the East Asian Olympic Games held in Shanghai, an "Exhibit of Buddhist Vegetarian Dietary Culture" was held by three of the major Buddhist temples of Shanghai—the Long Hua, the Jing An, and the Jade Buddha. In this exhibit, over 200 vegetarian dishes were displayed for public viewing and sampling on the part of both local inhabitants and foreign visitors, enabling all to experience how delectable a purely vegetarian diet can be.

"Vegetarian Feasts" or "Ch'ia," an important aspect of social-religious life among Chinese Buddhists, continue to be observed among Chinese everywhere, both on religious festivals and in commemoration of the dead. As has been noted, wherever there are large Chinese communities throughout the world, a minority of Buddhist vegetarians will exist— hence, the presence of one or more Chinese vegetarian restaurants. Indeed, both abroad and in China itself, Chinese Buddhists help to propagate vegetarianism through operating vegetarian restaurants. Not infrequently, they view this endeavour in terms of a "mission" to mankind and its achievement of a positive karma through kindness and non-violence directed towards animal beings.

In Singapore, where over half of the population is Chinese, many of whom are Buddhists, both Chinese and East Indian vegetarian restaurants abound, and a Mr. Koh Kok Keng, a Chinese Buddhist, is extremely prominent in vegetarian affairs and promotion. Even in Australia, Chinese Buddhists operate restaurants which provide high quality vegetarian fare for the general public, there being such eating-places in the cities of Perth and Adelaide as well as in other urban centres. The same is true of many cities with large Chinese communities in the United States and Canada.

While such restaurants are often adjuncts of temples or monasteries in China or Taiwan, elsewhere, they are usually run by devout Buddhist lay people. In order to understand the significance of such establishments, it is necessary to be cognizant of the importance of eating and banqueting in Chinese social and family life, particularly to commemorate family and individual events pertaining to both the living *and the dead.* Thus, Chinese vegetarian restaurants not only serve as ordinary eating places for Chinese

Buddhists, but as places where elaborate vegetarian banquets are held on major festivals as well as on anniversaries commemorating the dead. Indeed, for Chinese Buddhists there is a particular connection between vegetarian banquets and the commemoration of the dead. It is to this end that, in some of these restaurants, at least in China and Taiwan, sand-filled bronze receptacles are placed near the doors. There, patrons may light sticks of incense for the dead prior to participating in a "bloodless banquet" commemorating the dead. Indeed, among Chinese Buddhists, there is, on the popular level, a very strong belief that a certain "merit" accrues to those who eat food which involves no animal suffering or death, and that this "merit" can be transferred to the spirits of the dead, thereby aiding them in the process of attaining a propitious "rebirth."

In the above phenomena and ideas, the continuing influence of the revered Chu-hung can be seen. Across the centuries, this 16th-century ethical leader and great apostle of the vegetarian way of life continues to inspire Chinese Buddhists everywhere, however small in number, to observe a strictly vegetarian diet and to engage in Life-Releasing acts and ceremonies. A wealthy Buddhist businessman in contemporary Hong Kong, for instance, year after year, in order to fulfill the ethical injunctions of Chu-hung, spends considerable sums on the purchase of entire nets-full of live fish from the fishermen who have just caught them. These fish are then released back into the sea with special rites and chants on the part of the Buddhist clergy.

Here, it is perhaps worth noting that just as in Chu-hung's own day, the release of animals by Chinese Buddhists today occurs exclusively through strictly legal means—namely, through the purchase of the animals in question from their captor or possessor.

No less significant for vegetarianism among the Chinese are the many small independent "Lay Buddhist Associations" in contemporary Taiwan. These are termed "Chai-chiao." Although they have in some cases evolved into something rather different from the originals, these associations are unquestionably the spiritual descendents of Buddhist lay associations founded by the revered Chu-hung in mainland China during the late 16th century.

In some cases, the practices of these organizations incorporate certain ancient Chinese traditions of "spirit-writing" with a dedication to vegetarianism and Non-Violence. All are devoted to the two latter. Many of the members of these associations are persons who have been healed of some particular illness or ailment after vowing themselves to a perpetual vegetarian diet. Their temples bear names such as "Repaying Kindness Chapel." Their cults center around Shakyamuni, the historical Buddha; Kwan-Yin, the Bodhisattva of Compassion; and Amito-Fo, the Buddha of the Western Paradise. The members term each other "vegetarian friends." Their ethics place a particular emphasis on non-violence, vegetarianism, and kindness to animals and people.

The part played by spirit-writing and trances among many such devotees may perhaps be seen as a natural development stemming from Chu-hung's "bloodless banquets" for the dead as well as his concept of the transference of merit to the dead through abstinence from animal flesh and through the compassionate release of animals whose lives would otherwise have been taken.

In connection with the example of Chinese Buddhist vegetarianism, it may be observed that a few Buddhist lay people in Theravadin Southeast Asia, particularly in Thailand and Cambodia are returning to Buddhism's original vegetarian ethic which has been preserved by the Chinese over the centuries. In all probability, the recent formation of vegetarian associations in places such as Bangkok is largely due to the influence of a few Mahayanist Chinese temples in these areas, where the Theravadin natives themselves often hold their feasts for the dead due to the Chinese Buddhist expertise at preparing the necessary vegetarian fare.

THE UNITED STATES

Rather surprisingly, the United States has, within the last 30 years, emerged as the western country with the largest vegetarian minority. There are, in fact, an estimated 7 to 9 million[76] vegetarians in the United States today! Perhaps the majority of these are not members of any vegetarian organization as such, although some are members of various religious groups which encourage the observance of a vegetarian diet.

While American vegetarianism was once almost entirely nutritional and health-oriented in basis, a recent survey notes that two-thirds of the respondents state that they follow a vegetarian diet because they do not believe that animals should be killed and eaten. In other words, their vegetarianism has an ethical as well as a nutritional and ecological basis.

There are many vegetarian groups, societies, and associations in the United States today. Some are sectarian and others are completely non-sectarian. The largest of these is VUNA or The Vegetarian Union of North America with which many smaller local vegetarian associations and societies throughout Canada and the United States are affiliated. This organization meets yearly and publishes a quarterly newsletter. Its goal is to promote a balanced and scientific vegetarian perspective which emphasizes ethics and ecology no less than health and nutrition. The leading figures of this organization include such diverse individuals as Keith Akers, author of *A Vegetarian Sourcebook* as well as former President of VUNA and current Secretary; Peter McQueen of Toronto, President of the organization; Jay Dinshah, a Jain vegan who is the publisher of *Ahimsa*; world-traveller Vic Forsythe of Southern California; Franciscan brother Ron Pickarski, renowned vegetarian chef; and Victoria Moran, popular authoress and a leader of the "Unity Movement." VUNA is affiliated with The International Vegetarian Union which has its headquarters in Chester, England. This organization has members throughout the world.

Vegetarian videos are available, although sometimes not easy to find. One which is entitled *Diet for a New America* by Jon Robbins is highly recommended. It may be noted that the meat industry has vehemently opposed this film and has thus far succeeded in preventing its being shown on public TV! A non-sectarian magazine, *The Vegetarian Times*, a commercial enterprize unconnected with any vegetarian organization, is widely available in libraries, newstands, and organic food stores throughout the US. It is chiefly devoted to providing vegetarian recipes and pertinent news items.

Perhaps nowhere else does vegetarianism encompass such an immense diversity of perspectives and religious points of view as in North America where vegetarians may be Chinese Buddhists, Seventh Day Adventists, followers of Pythagoras or Gandhi, Roman Catholics, Humanist-oriented atheists, Jews, adherents of the Vedanta Society or the Krishna Consciousness Movement as well as just about any religious or non-religious group imaginable. Fundamentalist-pentecostalist Christians, who oppose the vegetarian way of life with a narrow intolerance and fanaticism, are, of course, major exceptions.

Particularly noteworthy has been the change in attitude towards vegetarianism that has developed among Roman Catholics in North America (and, to some extent, elsewhere) since Vatican II with its endorsement of a more liberal and tolerant viewpoint as well as a progressive Humanist ethic in many areas of life. As the new reformed Catholicism has veered sharply away from the intolerance and bigotry of its past, vegetarianism has ceased to be viewed as the "bete-noir" that it was in Roman Catholic circles in North America.

Thus, the idea that behind every vegetarian (excepting Trappists) lurks some sort of "heretic"—a Bogomil, Cathar, Gnostic, Manichean, or whatever—is no longer prevalent among Roman Catholics, either lay or clerical. Consequently, a new attitude has developed in more liberal Catholic circles in which vegetarianism is no longer "persona non-grata."

A prominent Franciscan brother, Ron Pickarski, who is also a professional vegetarian chef, is an outstanding example in this respect. He has, during the last decade become well-known in vegetarian circles for his vegetarian activism and widespread promotion of vegetarianism in many spheres of American life. Not only is he the author of an exceptionally fine vegetarian cookbook, *Friendly Foods*, but he has succeeded in pressuring various major airlines into carrying at least one vegetarian entree for their potentially vegetarian passengers as well as persuaded many school cafeterias to increase the availability of vegetarian dishes. He has also tirelessly lectured on the health and nutritional aspects of vegetarianism and promoted gourmet vegetarian cuisine as a means of enticing people to adopt a vegetarian diet. All in all, his services to the vegetarian cause are outstanding.

Nor is Brother Ron Pickarski the only Catholic vegetarian activist in North America. An editorial in the April 19/91 issue of the *National Catholic Reporter* endorses vegetarianism as a "preferable" mode of diet. The article takes a chiefly ecological stance, but nevertheless touches on ethical integrity (see the newsletter of the Vegetarian Union of North America, April/91, p. 6). Not to be viewed as representing, in an "official" capacity, the Roman Catholic Church the *National Catholic Reporter* is, of course, only a Catholic lay publication. That such views can today be openly promoted in any any

Catholic publication is commendable, but one need not hold one's breath for the emergence of a vegetarian pope or any official endorsement of vegetarianism on the part of a synod of bishops!

Long-time contributors to the advancement of vegetarianism in North America, the Seventh Day Adventists continue their tireless research into the medical and nutritional aspects of the vegetarian diet at the Loma Linda University and Medical Centre at Loma Linda, California, as well as the promotion of the vegetarian way of life among their members.

It may be noted, too, that an increasing number of prominent Americans are practicing vegetarians. Jerry Brown, a former Governor of California, maverick Democratic political leader, and notable Humanist who spent several years in India attending the ill and dying at a shelter run by Mother Teresa, is said to be a vegetarian.

CANADA

As for Canada, the vegetarian movement continues to grow there, just as it does throughout the world. The oldest continuously existent vegetarian organization in Canada is the Toronto Vegetarian Association or TVA, which was founded in 1945. This organization has grown from 18 members at its inception to some 600 today! Originally, its orientation was essentially ethical, that is, based upon man's ethical obligation to interact with the animal world in a kindly and compassionate fashion. During the 70s, the TVA also began to emphasize the health and ecological aspects of vegetarianism. For much of its existence, the Toronto Vegetarian Association was guided by Barbara Jackson who has been named "Honourary Founding President." She died in February 1992 at the age of 95, her great age being viewed by many as the natural result of her lifelong vegetarian diet!

During the 1950s and 60s, many vegetarian groups sprang up in other parts of Canada as well, although Toronto has remained the centre or nucleus of the vegetarian movement in Canada. Today, non-affiliated individual vegetarians as well as those who are affiliated with specific vegetarian groups or associations exist from Montreal to Victoria B.C., and from Halifax (the Maritime city with the largest number of vegetarians) Nova Scotia to Ottawa. There are even some vegetarians in Saskatchewan and in the Northwest Territories! The largest number, however, are found in the Provences of Ontario, Quebec, and British Columbia—in all of which there are ample vegetarian food outlets and restaurants, at least in the major cities. The most recent vegetarian group to come into existence in Canada is one which was formed in Fredricton, New Brunswick in 1992.

Rather curiously, there is no national vegetarian association or coalition in Canada, although some groups, such as the TVA are prominent participants in the Vegetarian Union of North America or VUNA, which includes both Canada and the United States. Indeed, Peter McQueen of Toronto is currently President of *both* the Toronto Vegetarian Association and the Vegetarian Union of North America! It may be noted that the well-known Canadian classical pianist, Anton Kwerti, is a dedicated vegetarian.

ISRAEL

We have already mentioned the Jewish contribution to the development of vegetarianism in North America in Chapter 16, also touching upon Jewish vegetarianism in general as well as a few of the leading personalities of the Jewish vegetarian movement of the 19th and 20th centuries.

There are many Israelis who are observant vegetarians, although no precise figures are available. While some of these are very low key and strictly private in their vegetarian observance, others are members of various vegetarian organizations. "The Israeli Vegetarian and Vegan Movement" is one of these. It sponsored the 29th World Vegetarian Congress which was held in Jerusalem and Tel Aviv in 1990. Said to consist mostly of older persons, this organization publishes an excellent vegetarian magazine in Hebrew.

"The International Jewish Vegetarian Society" or IJVS also has many Israeli members and a major chapter in Jerusalem. The members of this group are mostly English-speaking and the roots and headquarters of the organization are in London, England. Its newsletter is published in English, and it is notably "activist" in orientation. Consisting mostly, but by no means entirely of the younger generation, the Jerusalem Chapter of the Society was organized by Caren Greenwood. It has approximately 110 members. Thanks to the efforts of the well-known vegetarian and ecological activist, Philip Pick*, who is over 80 years old and is the President of the Society in London, an entire building has been acquired for the Jerusalem Chapter of the International Jewish Vegetarian Society. It is in the centre of Jerusalem in the Rehov Balfour, in near proximity to the Great Synagogue, Hechal Shlomo. It is intended to eventually transfer the vegetarian outreach and educational programmes of the Society to Jerusalem from their present London base. The Society emphasizes both the ethical and ecological basis of a vegetarian diet from within Jewish law and tradition.

THE UNITED KINGDOM

In England, the land where the modern vegetarian movement of the West was born, vegetarianism continues to thrive. Given the vegetarian fervour of Victorian times, one might have expected that a majority of the British population would be vegetarians by now. Unfortunately, this is not the case. Actually, only 3.6 million people or 7% of the total British population are known to be vegetarians today. It is generally felt, however, that a more realistic figure covering all persons in the UK who observe a vegetarian diet, including the large number who remain unconnected with any vegetarian organization, would be something more than twice that many, or around 16%.

The headquarters of the main British vegetarian organization, The Vegetarian Society of the UK, are located in Cheshire, England. There, too, are the headquarters of The International Vegetarian Union, which has members worldwide. The Vegetarian Society of the UK exists throughout Great Britain where, according to Maxwell Lee, the Honourable Secretary of the Society, a "massive growth of interest has occurred during the last few years." Among other contributing factors, a severe outbreak of the "mad cow disease" may have sparked an increased interest in vegetarianism from a purely health and disease-prevention angle.

The Vegetarian Society of the UK is very much involved in the active promotion of Ahimsa, which is to say peace and non-violence on a worldwide basis in all spheres of life, thus revealing the powerful influence of Gandhi as well as the continuance of the Brit-

* Now (1993) dead.

ish tradition of placing vegetarianism within the context of broader Humanist concerns. Needless to say, the Society encourages co-operation between all national, ethnic, racial, and religious groups.

One of the most remarkable facts concerning contemporary vegetarianism in the UK is the number of children and young people involved in it, not only as observant vegetarians, but also in terms of being members of "Vegetarian Clubs" in the schools. According to Maxwell Lee, 8% of all British youth between 11 and 18 years old are actively involved in the vegetarian movement. The extent of this interest is revealed in the fact that the Vegetarian Society of the UK receives up to 1,000 letters per week from interested young people in the schools. Furthermore, the Society has 4 full-time employees engaged in constantly visiting schools, both public and private, to propagate vegetarian outreach programs and give vegetarian presentations consisting of lectures, slides, and videos. These include both the ethical and nutritional aspects of vegetarianism, all within the context of broader Humanist social concerns. The Vegetarian Society of the UK has even succeeded in persuading some 45% of the schools at all levels to provide students with a choice of at least one vegetarian entree each day.

Unlike many other countries, including a number which claim to be "democratic," the United Kingdom is a living manifestation of genuine democratic enlightenment in that it allows educational programs involving the promotion of the vegetarian way of life to be brought into the schools themselves. Thus, *in the UK, the rights of young people to be exposed to alternative ethical and nutritional values are respected. So too, are their rights to think for themselves* and adopt the vegetarian way of life as a positive step forward towards a non-violent, more humane and health-oriented world dedicated to the weal of all sentient beings, *both human and animal.*

It was in Cheshire, England, at the headquarters of the Vegetarian Society of the UK that the European Vegetarian Congress was held in 1991. The majority of European countries and ethnic groups were represented, including even many among whom vegetarianism is infrequent.

AUSTRALIA AND NEW ZEALAND

Even in such major meat-producing and consuming areas as Australia and New Zealand, vegetarianism not only exists, but continues to expand. Adelaide might well be termed the centre of Australian vegetarianism. There, a Vegetarian Society has existed for some 40 years under the energetic leadership of Emma "Mick" Fearnside, who continues to carry on the Theosophist tradition of vegetarianism established by Annie Besant, but little observed by Theosophists today.

Perth is also an active centre of vegetarianism. In both Perth and Adelaide, the presence of devout Chinese Buddhists enhances the composition of the vegetarian community-at-large, and also provides both cities with excellent Chinese vegetarian restaurants. There are also small vegetarian organizations in Melbourne, Sidney, and elsewhere. The Australian vegetarian groups are quite local in scope and do not form a nationwide organization.

In New Zealand, a Vegetarian Society has been in existence in Aukland since 1942. As for other relatively nearby lands, it may be noted that, according to Maxwell Lee, in the July/92 newsletter of the International Vegetarian Union, new vegetarian societies have recently come into existence in both the Philippines and Japan.

18. Vegetarianism As a Way of Life Today and the Need for a Vegetarian "Ecumenism"

Fortunately, it is no longer possible for a bigoted predjudiced element of the public to dismiss vegetarianism as "faddist" and "irrational," as a "crank philosophy of diet" to be tolerated only as a "drole" and "absurd aberration." To the contrary, vegetarianism is today a respectable way of life, followed by millions of people who subscribe to many diverse spiritual and philosophical perspectives throughout the world. *Above all, it should be made clear that vegetarianism is not simply a matter of dietary preference.* Rather, it is a way of life which, in a broader context, is intimately bound up with the philosophy and ethics of Non-Violence as well as the hoped-for development and emergence of a higher civilization. On a more immediate level, vegetarianism involves living in harmony with Nature and maintaining a compassionate regard for and interaction with the animal world. Furthermore, vegetarianism is today viewed by the majority of its advocates as essential to the maintenance of good health, both physical and mental.

During this century, vegetarians have, in fact, grown into a sizable minority throughout much of the world. The ludicrous myth of the "pale-faced," "sickly," "non-virile" male vegetarian has long since been exposed as an absurd fantasy. The enormous increase in "natural," "organic," and health food stores in the last 40 years gives some indication of the extent to which vegetarians and vegetarianism have become part of mainstream western life. Meat-eating is no longer *the* socially-prescribed mode of diet demanded by unthinking custom. A number of diverse and extremely persuasive vegetarian perspectives exist, and the entire vegetarian rationale has become firmly grounded within a broad framework of ethics, nutrition, disease prevention, ecology, and aesthetics.

Not insignificant is the fact that vegetarianism receives the full endorsement of many prominent medical authorities. "The Physician's Committee for Responsible Medicine," headed by Dr. Neal Barnard, for instance, strongly recommends a strictly vegetarian diet as one to be preferred in terms of both nutritional value and disease prevention.

Although many contemporary vegetarians are not members of any particular religious organization, more than a few even subscribing to a Humanist-oriented atheism or agnosticism, many others are the adherents of specific spiritual paths deriving from one or another of the major world religions. In this respect, it is important for us to realize that whether or not we agree with the particular religious perspectives or teachings of any specific spiritual group or school of thought, *if* that group advocates a vegetarian diet for whatever reason, it contributes to the vegetarian movement in general and thus to a more harmonious, compassionate, and civilized world.

As we have previously noted, many different elements enter into the vegetarian rationale and the maintenance of a vegetarian diet in the world today. Firstly, there is what *should be* civilized man's basic ethical repulsion towards contributing to the suffering, torture, and killing of innocent animal beings who have every right to enjoy their lives without being subjected to barbaric human cruelty. Indeed, it might be said that many vegetarians perceive the observance of a vegetarian diet in terms of a moral duty or responsibility towards the animal world.

Secondly, there is the matter of health and nutrition. While not everyone who eats animals is notably unhealthy, the chances are that they *might be so*; that they are, in fact, *less healthy*, at least in some respects, than those who follow a diet which strictly excludes all forms of animal flesh.

Thirdly, most persons who observe a vegetarian diet, feel a decided aesthetic revulsion to both the idea and reality of eating the dismembered corpses of animals, however disguised by packaging, culinary trickeries, or cleverly-contrived sauces. In other words, they are repelled by the barbaric grossness of the matter.

Fourthly, there are numerous ecological reasons* to propagate and maintain a vegetarian diet.

* For a discussion of the ecological basis of vegetarianism, see Keith Akers' excellent study, *A Vegetarian Sourcebook.* Vegetarian Press. Denver, 1989. Pt. II, Chapters 9-16.

Fifthly, a vegetarian diet should be part of the "lifestyle" of everyone who seeks to live in harmony with Nature. Such a state can be attained only through not harming other animal beings. To cause the suffering and death of one's animal brethren is no less disruptive and violent to the harmony of natural being than to cause the suffering and death of another human being or to support the irrationality of aggressive wars. Such actions set in motion negative karmic effects which can extend throughout the whole of life and many cycles of being.

The reader will have observed that the present study does not include the issue of "animal rights" as such, but only touches on this subject in connection with the ethical basis of vegetarianism as well as what was in the ancient world the closely-related matter of opposition to animal sacrifice.

Here, it is perhaps not out of order to note that many vegetarians concerned with animal welfare feel that those animal rights activists who engage in lawless and anarchic actions which alienate the general public are something of a deterrent to the weal of the animals with whose well-being they claim to be concerned. What is needed in respect to animal rights is action *through strictly legal channels!* These might include well-presented public lectures as well as diverse presentations via the numerous communications media available, all to the end of enlightening the public. The traditional Chinese Buddhist method of open purchase of animals and the liberation or preservation of them in pleasant circumstances in order to save them from a cruel death might also serve as a model today.

It is sometimes claimed that a large scale adoption of a vegetarian diet would be extremely disruptive of the whole earthly economy. Thus, vegetarians must be ready with alternatives, both in terms of jobs and of the development of new vegetarian food industries. This serious challenge must be faced by all who advocate a vegetarian diet. It is for all vegetarians to seek new and creative sollutions to this problem, suggesting as well, means by which they could could be implemented. Part of the answer, of course, simply lies in a vast increase in the production of various soy bean and other high protein vegetable, grain, and nut products. In all this, there is considerable room, as well, for the exercise of human inventiveness. While dairy products would continue to fill important dietary needs, the so-called "dairy industry" itself would undergo certain major changes and transformations inasmuch as it would no longer exist in conjunction with the "meat industry." Needless to say, the animals involved would be treated with the respect and kindliness that they deserve, not only as animal beings, but out of particular gratitude for the many delectable milk products with which they enrich the human diet and cuisine. As for sheep, there is no reason whatever that they would not continue to be raised for wool, so long as they were treated respectfully in a kindly fashion. Needless to say, the methods used to obtain the wool would be revolutionized, so as to remove all traumatic qualities from the process and introduce a gentleness of demeanor which would preserve the animals from all manner of stress.

As Keith Akers, a former President of the Vegetarian Union of North America, has pointed out, what is needed today is a "vegetarian ecumenism" which would serve as a unifying factor to transcend all differences of specific philosophical or religious outlook. Hopefully, even those religious groups whose promotion of vegetarianism normally is set exclusively within the framework of their own particular beliefs, could be persuaded to participate on a broader level. In short, what is needed is for *all* vegetarians to work together in order to enlighten the public-at-large and effectively promote the Vegetarian Way of Life on a non-sectarian basis, eventually facilitating the coming into existence of a world wherein vegetarianism is the "norm" in a highly diversified human society based on the principle of *Ahimsa*.

Reference Notes*

1. see p. 154 (57)
2. p. 82 (57)
3. p. 82 (57)
4. p. 38 (53)
5. see (57)
6. see (50)
7. p. 123 (32)
8. p. 219 (37)
9. p. 212 (37)
10. p. 218 (37)
11. p. 221 (37)
12. p. 219 (37)
13. p. 215 (37)
14. p. 264 (27)
15. see (15)
16. see p. 86 (12)
17. see (50)
18. p. 3 (53)
19. p. 427 (53)
20. p. 429 (53)
21. p. 339 (53)
22. p. 519 (53)
23. see (4)
24. see (56)
25. p. 548 (56)
26. p. 550 (56)
27. p. 88 (56)
28. p. 551 (56)
29. p. 551, 553 (56)
30. see (55)
31. see (54)
32. see (73)
33. p. 181 (57)
34. p. 146 (57)
35. p. 148 (57)
36. p. 175 (57)
37. p. 86 (57)
38. p. 86 (57)
39. p. 82 (57)
40. p. 26 (49)
41. see pp. 237-242 (9)
42. p. 238 (9)
43. see p. 60 (14)
44. p. 229 (87)
45. see (41)
46. p. 74 (86)
47. p. 74 (86)
48. p. 233 (82)
49. p. 289 (43)
50. see p. 23 (72)
51. see (55)
52. see (29)
53. see (29), (72)
54. for further information on Cheyne, see (78)
55. see (69)
56. see p. 87 (69)
57. p. 95 (69)
58. p. 84 (69)
59. see (3)

* The numbers in parentheses refer to the numbers which appear before the books listed in the Bibliography, in other words, to the reference sources.

60. see p. 3 (71)
61. p. 9 (65)
62. p. 13 (65)
63. see (83)
64. p. 584 (64)
65. p. 37 (5)
66. see p. 9, 17 (78)
67. p. 18, 78 (78)
68. p. 281, 277 (45)

69. p. 274 (45)
70. p. 322 (45)
71. p. 286 (45)
72. p. 287 (45)
73. see (70)
74. see p. 234 (36)
75. see p. 234, 235 (36)
76. see (59)
77. see (59)

Bibliography

(1) Akers, Keith. *A Vegetarian Sourcebook.* The Nutrition, Ecology, and Ethics of a Natural Foods Diet. Vegetarian Press. Denver, Colo., 1989.

(2) Ashe, Geoffrey. *Gandhi.* Stein and Day. New York, 1968.

(3) Axon, William E. *Shelley's Vegetarianism.* An address given at a meeting of the Shelley Society and printed by the same. London, 1891. Reprinted by Haskill House, 1971.

(4) Barrow, R. H. *Plutarch and His Times.* Indiana University Press. Bloomington and London, 1967.

(5) Callahan, North. *Flight from the Republic.* Bobbs-Merrill & Co. New York, 1967.

(6) Cameron, Alister. *The Pythagorean Background of the Theory of Recollection.* George Banta Publishing Co. Menasha, Wis., 1938.

(7) Ch'en, Kenneth. *Buddhism in China.* Princeton University Press. Princeton, N. J., 1965.

(8) ———— . *The Chinese Transformation of Buddhism.* Princeton University Press. Princeton, N. J., 1973.

(9) Clement of Alexandria. *The Instructor.* Book II, p. 237-242. In the Ante-Nicene Fathers. Alexander Roberts and James Donaldson, editors. Christian Literature Co., Buffalo, 1885.

(10) Cooper, Stephen. *The Thought of Leo Tolstoy in Contemporary Counterculture.* Thesis C 787 in the Archives Library of the University of Oregon, Eugene.

(11) *Dictionary of National Biography.* Many volumes, various editors. Oxford University Press. Oxford and London, from 1885 on. Contains biographical material on prominent English persons, some of whom played a leading role in British vegetarianism.

(12)   Dombrowski, Daniel A. *The Philosophy of Vegetarianism.* University of Massachusetts Press. Amherst, 1984. A major study of the subject as pertaining to ancient Greece and Rome.

(13)   Driver, Christopher. *The British at Table, 1840-1980.* Hogarth Press. London, 1983.

(14)   Eissler, K. *Leonardo Da Vinci.* International Universities Press. New York, 1961.

(15)   *Encyclopedia Britannica,* 1911 Edition. See for articles on prominent vegetarian figures of the Classical Greco-Roman world, such as Plutarch.

(16)   *Encyclopedia of Religion.* Vol. 6, Mircea Eliade. Macmillan. New York, 1987. See for the "Golden Age."

(17)   *Encyclopedia of Religion and Ethics.* 13 volumes. James Hastings, ed. T. and T. Clark. Edinburgh, 1908.

(18)   *Food and Foodways.* Vol. 2, No. 1, 1987. Haywood Publishing Co. London and New York, 1987.

(19)   Galinsky, Karl. *Ovid's Metamorphosis.* University of California Press. Berkeley, 1975.

(20)   Gandhi, Mahatma. *Collected Works.* The Publications Division of the Government of India. Delhi, 1958.

(21)   ———. *Complete Writings.* Includes his *Autobiography* (1969), *The Moral Basis of Vegetarianism* (1959), and *Diet and Reform* (1964). Navajivan Publishing House. Ahmedabad, India, varied dates, many volumes.

(22)   ———. *The Story of My Experiments with Truth.* Public Affairs Press. Washington, D. C., 1960.

(23)   Geffcken, Johannes. *The Last Days of Greco-Roman Paganism.* North Holland Publishing Co. Amsterdam, New York, and Oxford, 1978.

(24)   Gernet, Jacques. *A History of Chinese Civilization.* Cambridge University Press. Cambridge, 1982.

(25)   Gibbon, Edward. *The Decline and Fall of the Roman Empire.* Heritage Press. New York, 1946. 3 vol.

(26) Glenn, Edgar. *The Metamorphosis. Essays.* University Press of America. New York, 1986.

(27) Goddard, Dwight. Editor. *A Buddhist Bible.* Extracts from various Buddhist Sutras. Dutton. New York, 1952. See p. 264-65 for passage in *Surangama Sutra* concerning meat-eating.

(28) Gombrich, Ernst. *Norm and Form. Studies in the Art of the Renaissance.* Includes his "Renaissance and the Golden Age." London, 1966.

(29) *Guardian, The.* London. May 21, 1713. See for Alexander Pope's article on man's ethical obligation to the animal world.

(30) Henderson, Archibald. *Bernard Shaw.* Appleton. New York and London, 1932.

(31) Hertzler, Joyce. *The History of Utopian Thought.* Macmillan. New York, 1926.

(32) Jaini, Padmanabh S. *The Jaina Path of Purification.* University of California Press. Berkeley, 1979.

(33) Jordan, David and Overmeyer, Daniel. *The Flying Phoenix. Aspects of Chinese Sectarianism in Taiwan.* Princeton University Press. Princeton, N. J., 1986.

(34) Kapleau, Roshi Philip. *To Cherish All Life. A Buddhist Case for Becoming Vegetarian.* Harper and Row. San Francisco, New York, London, and Sydney, 1982.

(35) Keith, Thomas. *Man and the Natural World, 1500-1800.* Allen Lane. London, 1983.

(36) Kresh, Paul. *Isaac Bashevis Singer. The Magician of 86th St.* Dial Press. New York, 1979.

(37) *Lankavatara Sutra, The.* D.T. Suzuki, trans. Routledge, Kegan Paul Ltd. London, 1956. This sutra is a major source of Buddhist ethical injunctions concerning a vegetarian diet. See particularly Sutra Section 244-259, p. 211-222.

(38) Levin Harry. *The Myth of the Golden Age in the Renaissance.* Indiana University. Bloomington, 1969.

(39)   Marcott, Anne, editor. *The Sociology of Food and Eating. Essays.* Gower. Hants, England, 1983.

(40)   McClain, Ernest G. *The Pythagorean Plato.* Nicolas Hays Ltd. Stony Brook, N.Y., 1978. An extremely erudite and esoteric study of Pythagoras and Plato, particularly in reference to the influence of the former on the latter.

(41)   McCurdy, Edward. *The Mind of Leonardo Da Vinci.* Dodd, Mead, and Co. New York, 1928.

(42)   ———— . *The Notebooks of Leonardo.* Braziller. New York, 1956.

(43)   Mennell, Stephen. *All Manners of Food.* Blackwell. Oxford and New York, 1985.

(44)   Mitchell, Sally, editor. *Victorian Britain.* Garland Pub. New York and London, 1988.

(45)   Moore, J. Howard. *The Unusual Kinship.* Charles Kerr and Co. Chicago, 1908.

(46)   More, Sir Thomas. *Utopia.* From the Ralph Robynson trans. of the original Latin in 1556. With an Introduction, notes, etc. by J. Rawson Lumby. The University Press. Cambridge, 1891.

(47)   Muntz, Eugene. *Leonardo Da Vinci—Thinker, Artist, and Man of Science.* Hardy, Pratt & Co. Boston, 1899. From the French.

(48)   *New York Times,* "Living Section." Sept. 14/1977. See article on Jewish vegetarianism entitled "When Keeping Kosher Isn't Kosher Enough."

(49)   Niven, Charles. *History of the Humane Movement.* Johnson. London, 1967.

(50)   Ovid. *The Metamorphosis.* Penguin Classics. London, 1970. See Book 15 for Pythagoras.

(51)   *The Oxford Classical Dictionary.* Clarendon Press. Oxford, 1970. N. G. Hammond, editor.

(52)   Payne, Robert. *The Life and Death of Mahatma Gandhi.* Dutton, New York, 1969.

(53) Philostratus. *The Life of Apollonius of Tyana.* English translation by F. Conybeare. Heinman. London, 1917.

(54) Plotinus. *The Ethical Treatises (Enneads).* 5 Vol. Porphyry's *Life of Plotinus* is contained in Vol. I. Philip Lee Warner. London, 1917.

(55) Plutarch. *The Lives. Marcus Cato.* Thomas North, trans. Dent. London, 1898-1908.

(56) ———— . *Moralia.* English trans. by Harold Chermiss and William Helmbold. Harvard University Press. Cambridge, Mass. and Heinman, London. 1957. Vol. 12—On the Eating of Flesh.

(57) Porphyry. *On Abstinence from Animal Food.* Trans. by Thomas Taylor. Centaur Press. London, 1965.

(58) Regan, Tom. *All That Dwell Therein.* University of California Press. Berkeley, 1982. For an extremely abstract presentation of the vegetarian point of view, see chapters 1 and 2 of this volume.

(59) *Register-Guard.* Eugene, Oregon. May 29/91. Section D, for an article on vegetarianism by Patrick Ercolano.
Also, April 9/91 for an article on the dietary recommendations of The Physician's Committee for Responsible Medicine, headed by Dr. Neal Barnard.

(60) Rhys-Davids, T. W. *Buddhist India.* Putnams. London, 1903. See for information concerning Asoka and his Edicts.

(61) Robbins, Jon. *Diet for a New America.* Stillpoint Press. N. H., 1987.

(62) Rollin, Bernard. *Animal Rights and Human Morality.* Prometheus Books. Buffalo, N. Y., 1981.

(63) Rowley, Francis. *The Humane Idea.* American Humane Education Society. Boston, 1912.

(64) Sabine, Lorenzo. *The American Loyalists or Biographical Sketches of Adherents to the British Crown in the Revolution.* Little, Brown. Boston, 1847.

(65) Salt, Henry. *Seventy Years Among the Savages.* Allen and Unwin. London, 1921.

(66) Sapontzis, S. F. *Morals, Reason, and Animals.* Temple University Press. Philadelphia, 1987.

(67) Schapiro, M. "Leonardo and Freud." *Journal of the History of Ideas.* No. 17: p. 147-78.

(68) Sheean, Vincent. *Mahatma Gandhi.* Knopf. New York, 1962.

(69) Shelley, Percy Bysshe. See *Shelley's Prose or The Trumpet of Prophecy.* David Clark, Editor. University of New Mexico Press, 1954. Contains Shelley's *Essay on the Vegetable System of Diet,* his *Vindication of Natural Diet,* and also quotes from *Queen Mab.*

(70) Singer, Isaac Bashevis. *Enemies, a Love Story.* Farrar, Straus. New York, 1971.

(71) Singer, Peter. *In Defense of Animals.* Basil Blackwell Inc. New York, 1985. Contains a worldwide list of vegetarian organizations.

(72) Sitwell, Edith. *Alexander Pope.* Norton. New York, 1962.

(73) Smith, Andrew. *Porphyry's Place in the Neo-Platonic Tradition.* The Hague, 1974.

(74) Stanley, Thomas. *Pythagoras.* London, 1687. Reprinted by the Philosophical Research Society. Los Angeles, 1976.

(75) *The Sunday Express,* London. October 12/1930. Shaw: "What I Eat and Why."

(76) Tolstoy, Leo. *Recollections and Essays by Leo Tolstoy.* The Tolstoy Society. Oxford University Press. Oxford, 1937. See particularly pp. 124-35.

(77) Tsuzuki, Chushchi. *Edward Carpenter, Prophet of Human Fellowship.* Cambridge University Press. Cambridge, 1980.

(78) Turner, James. *Reckoning with the Beast. Animals, Pain, and Humanity in the Victorian Mind.* John Hopkins University Press. Baltimore and London, 1980.

(79) Vasari. *Lives.* Vol 2. Edited by E. Blahfeld and A. Hopkins. Scribners. New York, 1897.

(80) Von Fritz, Kurt. *Pythagorean Politics in Southern Italy.* Columbia University Press. New York, 1940.

(81) *VUNA Views.* The reader is advised to see "VUNA Views," the quarterly newsletter of the Vegetarian Union of North America, for extensive information concerning Vegetarianism in North America and throughout the world. Subscription-membership costs $16.00 per year and includes the "International Vegetarian Union" newsletter (headquarters in Cheshire, England) which keeps readers updated on the Vegetarian Movement in the UK, continental Europe, India, and elsewhere. For information write to: Vegetarian Union of North America, P. O. Box 9710, Washington, D. C. 20016 or: Keith Akers, P. O. Box 6853, Denver, Colorado 80206

(82) Wacher, John. *Roman Britain.* J. M. Dent and Sons Ltd. London and Toronto, 1978.

(83) Winston, Stephen. *Jesting Apostle.* (Shaw). Dutton. New York, 1957.

(84) Wright, Arthur F. *Buddhism in Chinese History.* Stanford University Press. Ca., 1959.

(85) Wynne-Tyson, Alfred. *Food for a Future.* An argument for vegetarianism on humane and ecological grounds. Sphere. London, 1976.

(86) Yu, Chun-fang. *The Revival of Buddhism in China.* Columbia University Press. New York, 1981. A major source in English for that all-important figure in Chinese Buddhist vegetarianism, the revered Chu-hung.

(87) Zubov, V. *Leonardo Da Vinci.* Harvard University Press. Cambridge, Mass., 1968.

Grateful acknowledgements are
extended to the following publishers:

(1) Arkana for quotations from the *Lankavatara Sutra*, trans. by D. T. Suzuki, reproduced by permission of Penguin Books Ltd., London.

(2) Centaur Press Ltd., Fonthill, West Sussex, England for quotations form Porphyry's *On Abstinence from Animal Food* as well as from J. Howard Moore's *Universal Kinship* and Henry Salt's *Seventy Years Among the Savages*, both recently reprinted by Centaur.

(3) Columbia University Press, N. Y. for quotations from *The Revival of Buddhism in China* by Chun-fang Yu.

(4) Harvard University Press, Cambridge, Mass. for quotations from Plutarch's *Moralia, Vol. 12* and from *Apollonius of Tyana* by Philostratus, the Loeb Classical Library.

(5) The University of New Mexico Press, Albuquerque for quotations from *Shelley's Prose or The Trumpet of Prophecy*, ed. by David Clark.

Appendix I

Alcott, Dr. William
Allinson, Dr.
Apollonius of Tyana
Aristus
Arnold, Sir Edwin
Asoka, Buddhist Emperor of
    India

Balzer, Eduard
Bentham, Jeremy
Besant, Annie
Buber, Martin
Buddha, the (Shakyamuni)

Carpenter, Edward
Celus
Cheyne, Dr. George
Chu-hung, the revered
Cocci, Dr. Antonio
Cowherd, William
Crates

Damas the Syrian
Da Vinci, Leonardo
Dichaearchus

Einstein, Albert
Empedocles

Epicetus
Evans, Joshua

Gandhi, Mahatma
Gompertz, Lewis
Graham, Sylvestor

Hesiod
Hierocles of Alexandria

Jackson, Barbara
Joynes, J. L.
Julia Domna, Empress of
    Rome

Kellog, Dr. John Harvey
Kellog, William K.
Kharaabati, J. Ermian
Kingsford, Anna

Lambe, Dr. William
Lu Yu-hsi
Lysis

Mahavira, Tirthankara
Manker, Sri J. N. ("Mankerji")
Mehta, Raychandbhai
Mehta, Sri Surendra

Note: It is possible that Plato and Socrates were both vegetarians, too, although there is no definite evidence.

Appendix II

SOME PROMINENT VEGETARIAN ACTIVISTS
OF THE CONTEMPORARY WORLD

Akers, Keith

Barnard, Dr. Neal

Bukovsky, Dr. Igor

Dinshah, Jay

Dombrowsky, Daniel

Fearnside, Emma "Mick"

Ferrier, Dr. Serge Reynauld de la

Gorelov, Anatoly

Greenwood, Caren

Kapleau, Roshi Philip

Koh Kok Keng

Lee, Maxwell

Luite, Kristina

McQueen, Peter

Mehta, Sri Surendra

Moran, Victoria

Pickarski, Br. Ron

Pribis, Dr. Peter

Robbins, Jon

Silva, G. A. de

Singer, Peter

Wang Chang Qing

Wingquist, Arne

Wolf, Jonathan

Index

A

Aesthetics, vegetarianism and, 23, 32, 40-41, 70-71, 76, 108
Africa, 108
Ahimsa, 14-15, 17, 21, 62, 83-86, 121, 127
Akers, Keith, 117, 125, 127
Alcott, Dr. William, 92
"All Union Vegetarian Society of Russia," 111
Animals and ethic,
    in Buddhism, 17-21, 60-63
    in Christianity, 46-49, 51
    in Hinduism, 13, 15, 17, 84
    in Jainism, 14-15
    in the teachings of Pythagoras and other Greco-Roman advocates of vegetarianism, 4, 6-9, 23, 26-27, 31-32, 35
    in Victorian and pre-Victorian England, 64-68, 74-76, 78-79, 83-84
    release of animals, 7, 57, 62-63, 73, 115, 126
    sacrifice of animals, 8, 11, 13, 17, 20, 26, 28-30, 34, 36, 81
Apollo and his cult, 4-5, 9, 30, 59
Apollonius of Tyana, 27-30
Aristus, 4
Arnold, Sir Edwin, 82
Asoka or Asokavardhana, Buddhist Emperor of India, 19-20
"Associazione Vegetarina Italiana," 106

B

Atheism and atheists, 14, 67, 69, 72, 76, 117, 125
Athens Academy, 50
Australia, 122

B

Baltzer, Eduard, 88
Barnard, Dr. Neal, 125
Bentham, Jeremy, 67
Besant, Annie, 96-97
Birds, 7, 57, 62, 75-76, 94, 102, 107
Bodhisattva Ideal, 21
Britain, vegetarianism in
    contemporary, 121-122
    Victorian Period and before, 64-82
    also see index entries for specific individuals
Buber, Martin, 100
Buddha, the Gautama (Shakyamuni), 17-19, 61
Buddhism, Chinese, 37-43, 60-63, 112-116
    influence on Chinese arts and culture, 40-41
    also see entries for China, vegetarianism in and for specific Buddhist Emperors listed in appendix
Buddhism, Japanese
    anomalies of vegetarian practice, 43-44
Buddhism, original Indian, 19-20, 42

Krishna Consciousness Movement, the
  its popularization of vegetarian diet, 98
Kwan-yin, Bodhisattva of Compassion and Patron of Animals, 40, 113, 115

L

Lambe, Dr. William, 72
Lankavatara Sutra, a primary source of vegetarian injunctions in Buddhism, 18-19
Latin America, vegetarianism in, 108-110
Lay Buddhist Movement, Chinese, 60-61, 63, 115
  also see Buddhism, Chinese and Chu-hung
Lee, the Hon. Maxwell (of Cheshire), 121
Lithuania, the Palanga Institute, 110
Loma Linda University and Medical Centre,
  its importance for vegetarian medical research, 118
Lorenzo de 'Medici and his Court, 53-55
Luite, Kristina (of Estonia), 110
Lysis, 11

M

Macrobiotic Movement
  not strictly vegetarian, 98
  its popularization of grains, sea vegetables, and soybean products, 98
Magna Graecia, 6

Mahavira, Tirthankara, 14-15
Mahayana Buddhism,
  see Buddhism, Chinese and Buddhism, Japanese
Manker International Foundation and Manker, Sri J. N., 107
Mauritius, recent formation of a vegetarian society, 108
McQueen, Peter—President of both VUNA and the TVA, 117, 119
Medicines from animals proscribed, 33, 39, 62
Mehta, Raychandbhai, 16, 84
Mehta, Sri Surendra, 107
"Merit," 61-62, 116
Metcalfe, William, 92
Metrocles, 23
Milk foods, 9, 15, 26, 77, 81, 84, 86, 126
Ming Dynasty, 60
Montaigne, Michel Eyquem de, 87
Moore, J. Howard, 94-95
Moran, Victoria, 117
More, Sir Thomas, 64
Morris, Rev. Francis, 75
"Moscow Tolstoy Society," the, 111
Moulon Foulon, Le, 105
Musonius, 24

N

"National Catholic Reporter," its endorsement of vegetarianism, 118
"Naturism" and vegetarianism, 32, 76-77, 92, 109
"Naturistas," 109